The S.H.T.F. Art of War

By

Jeffrey Merlin Olson

The S.H.T.F. Art of War.

By Jeffrey M. Olson

ISBN-13: 978-1495326578

Cover art and design © 2014 Jeffrey M. Olson

Text © 2014 Jeffrey M. Olson

Copyright © Jeffrey M. Olson 2014; all rights reserved.

Without limiting the rights under copyright reserved above, no part of this publication may be reproduced, stored in or introduced into a retrieval system, or transmitted, in any form or by any means (electronic, mechanical, photocopying, recording or otherwise), without the prior written permission of the copyright owner.

The scanning, uploading and distributing of this book via the internet or any other means without the permission of the publisher, is illegal and punishable by law. Please purchase only authorized print and electronic editions and do not participate in or encourage electronic piracy of copyrightable materials.

This book is for educational and entertainment purposes only.

The author and publisher do not in any way condone illegal activities of any kind.

All advice in this book is for entertainment and educational purposes only, and the author cannot be held responsible for the use of information provided in each particular legal context.

Check your local, state, and federal laws regarding everything related in this book and obey laws in which they apply to you.

For more articles by Jeffrey M. Olson visit:

www.shtfartofwar.com

You can also find him on Facebook

https://www.facebook.com/shtfArtOfWar

To my loving wife Traci.

The wonderful woman who cured me of my notoriously vicious and intemperate disposition.

You my dear, are my Androcles.

"There is only one tactical principle which is not subject to change. It is to use the means at hand to inflict the maximum amount of wound, death, and destruction on the enemy in the minimum amount of time."

- General George Patton Jr.

Table of Contents

Introduction 1

From the Author to the Reader 5

Part 1 The Apocalyptic Criminal Warlord 10

What is your Disaster Personality? 10

Indoctrinated for Peace 14

Societal Collapse 15

Eat the Rich 17

Student of War 20

The Rise of a Leader 21

Know your Enemy (21 traits and skills of an Apocalyptic Warlord) 22

1. Physically Tough 23
2. Mean & Nasty 23
3. Bad Reputation 24
4. Enhanced Interrogations 25
5. Student of Basic Warfare..................... 25
6. The Strategies of War 26

7. Intelligence Gathering 26
8. Nomadic Life Style 26
9. Soft Targets 27
10. Inner Circle 29
11. Body Guards.................................. 29
12. The Complaint Department 30
13. Spoils of War 30
14. Take a Chill Pill...............................31
15. Bad Apples.................................... 31
16. Maintaining Order............................ 31
17. Too many mouths to feed 32
18. Post Apocalyptic Commerce 32
19. Post Apocalyptic Romance 33
20. Elusive 34
21. Betrayer.. 35

<u>What can you do to defend yourself from these marauders?</u>.. 36

<u>Post Apocalyptic Side Arm</u> 37

<u>The Main Battle Rifle</u>.............................. 40

The Flow of Crime ………………………….. 41

Part 2 How to be a FEMA Camp Hero

………………………………….…………. 43

Inalienable Rights …………………………….. 45

Martial Law ………………………………… 49

Executive Order List ………………………… 51

Pick a winning SHTF survival team …………... 55

Asset or Liability ……………………………… 57

Is FEMA right for you? ……………………… 59

The Benefits of a FEMA Camp ……………....…61

How to prepare for your FEMA camp stay ……. 64

Twenty Five Refugee Rules for FEMA camp Survival ……………………………………….. 69

Part 3 SHTF Traffic Sucks ……….. 79

Part 4 The Lost Art of Scavenging……. 88

Highly Recommended Items to include in your apocalyptic scavenger survival kit ……………. 88

Ten Everyday Survival rules…………………. 89

Activities toward Staying Alive ………………… 90

The best locations for scavenging............. 91

Tools of the scavenger ....…......… 93

Bring a scavenging buddy ....….. 94

Drones 94

Part 5 Apocalyptic Professions...... 95

A quick word about food storage ...….....… 107

Conclusion 109

About the Author ....….. 111

The S.H.T.F. Art of War

Introduction

LIFESAVING ADVICE FOR FERVENT SURVIVALISTS

—Dr. Carson Gardner, January 2014

I have some *lifesaving advice for fervent survivalists*—we'll *acronymize* that to L.A.F.F.S., to be trendy. Just for L.A.F.F.S., pay attention…*now*…

I have known Jeff for well over a decade. He doesn't work for me, but he sort of works because of me; or at least because of the initials behind my name. He really doesn't need *anyone else's initials* to make him competent, thoughtful and responsible. But he doesn't seem to mind the technicality much, in practice. I have never swung a hammer and sweated beside Jeff at his forge, packed a bug-out bag *exactly* his way or traded favorite firearms with him on the shooting range. Even so, it's easy for me to recognize that Jeff exudes a quiet, unselfconscious, well-anchored internal order; as free of pompous pride as he is of waffling wuss-itude.

Also, Jeff understands human nature and knows how to manage people, especially people under fire by various forms of hazard—self-generated or otherwise. He has made his mistakes and learned his lessons; though he makes no bones

Jeffrey M. Olson

about the fact that he is always, and in all situations, still learning.

He respects only those who have earned, *and continue to earn*, his respect. He trusts dead philosophers more than live hucksters—at least the dead philosophers who agree with his powerfully-tuned internal compass.

Jeff displays honestly impatient anger when presented with bureaucratic bullshit or asinine apathy; but he has learned to control that scorching heat generated at such times, deftly redirecting it toward brilliantly-useful illumination.

While he is unashamedly non-religious, he is also one of the few individuals with whom I am comfortable talking spiritual philosophies— especially the ones that are earth-born and earth-grown. Jeff neither pulls his philosophical punches nor brandishes rhetorical brass knuckles. If he can be said to devoutly worship anything, it is the living and breathing, teaching and testing **land** beneath his own feet—and the **knowledge** it imparts when its whisper is heard and understood.

Jeff places ultimate value on common sense; real-deal ditch education; hard-but-efficient work; honest humility; practical wisdom from life's circles, seasons and rhythms; promises made only to be kept and truths (not *The Truth*, just truths) that can be tested and then trusted like good, well-tempered-and-rightly-quenched iron.

In fact, I have given him the name, *Biiwaabik Inini*, which in Ojibwemowin means *man of iron*. Good, well-earned name.

Jeff knows a great truth, perhaps the most useful truth any human being ever admitted knowing: Without practical two-way connection to something greater *and better* than themselves, human beings are merely the worst, most malignantly dangerous *parasites* that ever slithered the face of Earth.

The whole purpose of life on earth for us humans turns out to be solely to metamorphose from parasites to symbionts, living in peaceful, responsible harmony with our patient and forgiving *Grandmother Earth*; honorably giving back *at least* as much as we get from the gift of life. So, it's no surprise that Jeff pays for the groceries by doing **E**mergency **M**isadventure **S**alvage.

Jeff believes in the "three questions" teaching.

When we each face death—alone—death asks only three questions of each human being:

1. **What is your name**?

2. **What do you have to say for yourself**?

3. **What have you done with your life**?

Jeff has some damn good answers to these questions.

Jeffrey M. Olson

So, just for L.A.F.F.S.,

(**L**IFESAVING **A**DVICE **F**OR **F**ERVENT **S**URVIVALISTS**)**

... shut up and listen to him.

The S.H.T.F. Art of War

From The Author To The Reader

Hello and thanks for buying this book.

If you've bought this book, I assume you understand what the acronym S.H.T.F. stands for. However, a wise man once said "When you **assume**, you make an ass out of you and me." Making an ass out of someone is not the way to make a first impression.

To avoid that awkward indignation, I'll give you a quick definition of what S.H.T.F. stands for: S.H.T.F. means Shit Hits The Fan; a term used by survivalists and preparedness minded people to describe a big disaster that leads to the total break-down of civilization and social order.

I will also give fair warning that you may not like or agree with everything I have to say. I'm respectfully unapologetic about that. I purposely wrote this book to push your mind into an uncomfortable way of thinking. If some of what I have to say rubs you the wrong way, then I have done what I set out to do: make you think. Like the old saying goes; "No Pain-No Gain."

I realize there are a lot of prepper and survival "how to" books out there on the market. In this book I won't bore you with detailed lists of survival gear, gardening or how to build a bug out location. There's plenty of free information on the web about those topics.

Jeffrey M. Olson

You'll find that I do briefly talk about firearms and food storage, but the main focus will be on the following 5 topics:

1. **The Apocalyptic Criminal Warlord**. This will cover the criminal element and how they will operate during a grid-down situation.

2. **How to be a FEMA Camp Hero**. This controversial section will cover how to prepare for and better endure a stay at a FEMA "recovery" camp.

3. **SHTF Traffic Sucks**. "This will help you know how, in a major disaster event, to deal with everyone else in the disaster area hitting the road to get out of the city—millions of other refugees spilling out into the countryside of rural America imagining it'll automatically be better out there.

4. **The Lost Art of Scavenging**. This will give you advice on how to scavenge on the remains of a collapsed society.

5. **Apocalyptic Professions**. This will introduce you to some post-apocalyptic professions; time tested trades that will help you survive and start your new post- apocalyptic career in an environment where the goods and services of modern society have become extinct.

I've worked hard to keep the following information streamlined and to the point. I created this book to

The S.H.T.F. Art of War

be a short, immediate-action type of work that could be read in one sitting. I did this because most of us are severe procrastinators. Most of us wait until the last minute to do anything.

Even when people have advanced warning of an impending winter storm or hurricane, the TV News routinely shows them running—last minute—to the stores for basic supplies. Humans, for the most part, are reactionary creatures and store shelves do not hold enough supplies for everyone.

In the event of a societal collapse, I believe this same procrastination phenomenon will happen when people suddenly find themselves needing knowledge on security and warfare. When your life suddenly depends on that knowledge, you're going to want it in a big damn hurry. Security is like air. You never think about it until you don't have it any more.

Can a society really collapse? I think the majority of people believe a complete societal collapse cannot realistically happen in the modern world. There are a lot of people who will think you're crazy for even entertaining the thought that tomorrow may be any different than today. However, just turn on the news today and you'll hear that crime is on the rise in the inner cities. Jobs are becoming scarce and job growth is stagnant. Politicians and Police are out of ideas on how to contain the growing drug and crime problems.

Jeffrey M. Olson

They are also scared of law abiding citizens being armed to protect themselves. The gap between the rich and the poor is becoming a not-so-grand canyon. Prisoners are being released early from prison because those prisons are extremely overcrowded. Corruption is rampant in government, corporate, and financial institutions. We have a population that is willfully ignorant and distracted by celebrities, sports, entertainment, and consumerism. Paychecks are smaller and taxes are up. All this looms at the same time as food and fuel prices are increasing.

Financial experts warn that the entire world is currently teetering on the inevitability of a worldwide economic collapse. The statements by financial gurus defining our current economic system as "mathematically guaranteed to fail" and "unsustainable" do not do a lot for my confidence. How's yours doing?

Economic and societal collapses are nothing new. History is filled with the ruins of once great civilizations. This collapse, however, will be different because it will be a worldwide collapse— in some sinister ways like a comet strike without the comet.

At this point, you would assume I'm consumed with bleak cynicism and grim pessimism. To the contrary, I'm much more optimistic than you would probably think. I look for opportunities in every situation and how best to take advantage of them.

The S.H.T.F. Art of War

I have high hopes and confidence that certain other individuals, across the world, with this same outlook can and will rise above and survive any crisis.

Even though I'm a rather positive fellow, I also never lose sight of the importance of planning for a worst-case scenario. A wise person plans for the worst and lives for the best.

With that being said, let's get started and take a look at the worst case scenario and examine what immediate dangers you'll be facing: **a scenario of a complete societal collapse that violently shoves our modern way of life into the dark ages.**

"To hell with them fellas. Buzzards gotta eat, same as worms."
— The Outlaw Josey Wales

Jeffrey M. Olson

Part 1

The Apocalyptic Criminal Warlord.

What is Your Disaster Personality?

The experts who've studied how people react and respond to life-and-death situations have come to the conclusion that we really don't know what our disaster personality is going to be. It may be far different than we think it will be.

This fascinated me. I decided to take an honest look at myself. What would be my disaster personality if there were a total collapse of society?

- My operational background is in military law enforcement. I've had training in guerilla warfare/counterterrorism operations.

- I've worked in the Middle East for private sector companies as a security contractor.

- I'm a student of ancient and modern warfare strategies.

- I've always been fascinated with religious cult leaders and how they control their followers.

The S.H.T.F. Art of War

- I believe in being prepared ahead of time. I do this to avoid having to venture out into the panicked masses in an emergency.

- I'm not anti-government and do not have a political agenda. However, it's frustrating to witness the corruption we see public officials engage in on a daily basis. Like most people, I think some of our elected officials could be doing a heck of a lot better job.

- I believe most people in America are sheep, just grazing their lives away on bad reality TV, sports, video games and media propaganda.

So even though I'm a law-abiding, productive member of society, my look into the apocalyptic mirror reveals that I have some of the ingredients needed to be an apocalyptic criminal warlord. We'll go over the whole list, below.

However, I currently have a moral compass and know my limitations. I'm middle aged and out of shape. I'm sure I'd be better suited to just being a third rate, semi-loyal, assistant to a henchmen of an apocalyptic warlord.

"All men would be tyrants if they could."
— *Daniel Defoe*

Jeffrey M. Olson

After thinking about this for awhile I became a bit unnerved. I started thinking about all the people who may be out there who are not productive members of society. I thought back to my time working as a security contractor and some of the scary individuals I knew.

I realized I had worked alongside and come into contact with some unsavory characters that had much more impressive tactical resumes than I do.

Some had ALL the ingredients needed to be an apocalyptic warlord. A few already had a following of minions to do their bidding.

These thoughts became even more unsettling when I realized that there's no shortage of people who have a feeling of bitterness towards authority and the civilized world.

The stark awareness of this disgruntled population became apparent early in 2013, when I saw a Facebook fan page making a hero out of the multiple-murder suspect, Chris Dorner. Over 16,000 people "liked" the page and were praising this suspected cop killer for fighting injustice and racism.

My guess is that there are hundreds of thousands of people who are disgruntled with their station in life. People hiding in plain sight, waiting and hoping for a Zombie Apocalypse to occur in the country; only then to rise up with their kill list and

The S.H.T.F. Art of War

exact their vengeance upon those they believe to have wronged them personally.

I decided to use my knowledge, experience and skills for good instead of evil. I wrote this book to alert the "good people" out there to what kind of dangers they will immediately encounter if an event happens that strips away the current rule of law.

I did this to help them better prepare for the savages who will be freely roaming the streets and countryside. I wanted to put out information that gets right at the heart of how the bad guys are going to operate in an environment without the rule of law to stop them.

To be honest, I almost didn't put this information out to the public. I felt the people who most needed to be aware of the dangers that will be knocking at their door during a time of great calamity would never read this book. I'd be giving out answers to people who hadn't even asked the question.

For the unaware, ignorance is bliss. What would be the point in writing an ignorance cure? Why waste my time and energy?

Then a beam of light cracked my dark, cold, pessimistic exterior and illuminated my moral compass. I thought if just one person reads this

Jeffrey M. Olson

material and can keep their family from harm, then I feel morally obligated to try.

"You may not be interested in war, but war is interested in you."
— *Leon Trotsky*

Indoctrinated for Peace

Possessing a rudimentary understanding of the brutal strategies for warfare in a peaceful, civilized society, is not needed nor is it encouraged on a day-to-day basis. We are taught from a very young age to avoid conflict and get along with our brother/sister/neighbor. We are forced to shake hands and "make nice" after a disagreement—which I happen to agree with. It's a good lesson, but it fails to address how to deal with those individuals who do not seek peace, love and understanding.

The act of defending yourself from an unprovoked attack in our schools is met with punishment:

In 2013, a 7-year old Colorado child was suspended from school for throwing an imaginary hand grenade on the playground;

A 6-year-old boy was suspended from an elementary school in Maryland for forming his fingers into a gun and saying "Pow";

In February of 2013, a 7-year old at a Delaware school was suspended for 2 days for chewing a pastry into the shape of a gun. That's right. A freaking pastry!

I could go on with ludicrous examples such as these. I think it's safe to say that the vast majority of Americans are not mentally equipped for the brutality of warfare. Our children are woefully unprepared for the harshness of life in a societal collapse:

"Perhaps the meek shall inherit the Earth, but they'll do it in very small plots . . . about 6' by 3'."
— *Robert A. Heinlein*

During a societal collapse without the rule of law, even the most basic knowledge of warfare will be invaluable to keeping you and your family safe:

"The true soldier fights not because he hates what is in front of him, but because he loves what is behind him."
— *G.K. Chesterton*

Societal Collapse

Historical fact shows that desperate people do very desperate things when life sustaining services, food and fuel stop coming into the area they live. I'd like to note that after Hurricane Sandy in 2012, fuel shortages and signs of a social breakdown began in less than 4 days. You must be aware that even in calm, peaceful times, there are predators living among us who know no depths to their depravity.

Jeffrey M. Olson

It's of great importance to know that even "regular" people show very different faces or mindsets when it comes to real life-and-death survival. A person's "survival personality" may be very different than even they think it can be when there isn't enough food to go around.

In the event of a complete societal collapse, where goods and services have stopped flowing throughout the country, there will be no 911. No Law Enforcement or Emergency Services to come to your aid. The constitution won't matter. There'll be no civil liberties, Bill of Rights or Geneva Convention to protect your human rights.

Bands of organized marauders and cutthroats will appear once they realize that there will be absolutely no consequences for their actions. They won't miss a step in taking advantage of an opportunity like this. They already live in this criminally-minded paradigm. They will act fast and have a head start. In the recent history of natural disasters, looters and criminals take advantage of these grid-down, chaotic situations in less than 24 hrs. The bigger the disaster, the more emboldened they become and the faster they strike:

When a tornado hit the rural town of Warroad, Minnesota with a population of less than 1,800, in May of 2011, the liquor store was robbed immediately after the storm had passed and several burglaries took place overnight.

The rule of fairness goes like this: *people won't play fair.* The more competitive a particular crisis environment is, the more the use of ruthless cheating strategies becomes commonplace.

Eat the Rich

Financial experts warn that the entire world is currently teetering on the inevitability of a worldwide economic collapse. More and more we hear statements by financial gurus defining our current system as "mathematically guaranteed to fail" and "unsustainable."

Edgar Rice Burroughs was right when he used the phrase, *"the thin veneer of civilization"* to describe mankind's condition in relation to his more fundamental savage makeup:

When the U.S. dollar collapses the people will be angry and looking to place blame for their misery. The disillusioned youth and angry workers will rise up against their betters.

The first to suffer will be the business owners and wealthy individuals in this country. The "Mob Rules" doctrine will be firmly in place.

"When the people shall have nothing more to eat, they will eat the rich."
— *Jean-Jacques Rousseau*

Mobs have a mind of their own. We hear in the news these days about "flash mobs." There are

Jeffrey M. Olson

two kinds of flash mobs. One is a group of people who assemble suddenly in a public place, perform an unusual and seemingly pointless act for a brief time, and then quickly disperse; often for the purposes of entertainment, satire and artistic expression. The other kind is for the purpose of *crime*. These mobs start with the intent of destruction, and/or lead to the actual destruction of private property; by rioting, violence and personal injury.

The latter mob type is the one we're concerned with here. We've all watched recent events on TV where the mobs turn to rioting and cause destruction after sporting events. It's estimated that over 100,000 people participated in the 1992 LA riots. Participants of that riot did so primarily over racial hatred not food.

But, in 3 days without eating, a person who's starving will have a complete change in psychological and sociological behavior. A primitive, primal-like behavior will emerge in such an individual. Need to feed will begin to overwhelm ethics, morals and lawfulness. The need to eat is a very powerful motivating force from which none of us are immune. Throughout history, there are many accounts of humans resorting even to cannibalism to survive in extreme circumstances.

It's easy for us to say that we would never resort to theft, looting, rioting, murder or cannibalism.

The S.H.T.F. Art of War

We confidently make such statements with a belly full of food and a full refrigerator. We make these statements knowing that there are stocked grocery stores and restaurants serving meals down the street.

In 1944, Dr. Andrew Keys conducted the "Great Starvation Experiment" at the University of Minnesota. He conducted this experiment to develop a rescue strategy for victims of the concentration camps of World War II. He studied the psychological and physiological effects of starvation on the human body. The results showed the participants suffered severe psychological trauma and side effects. They lost the ability to concentrate and form rational thought. They lost the ability to make sound judgments and comprehend the world around them. They had severe mood swings, were easily irritated and were always angry. Dreams and thoughts of cannibalism were reported by all the test subjects. There were also acts of self mutilation, threats of murder and theft.

It's important to note that these test subjects were volunteers of sound body and mind. Their caloric intake was only reduced to half of their normal daily diet and they were still eating two meals a day during the experiment. They knew when the experiment would begin and end. They also knew they would not die during the study.

Jeffrey M. Olson

This begs the question of what will starving mobs of people do when there is no food in the stores and the rule of law is absent? What atrocities will they commit when there is no fear of consequence for anyone's action?

"The mob is the mother of tyrants."
—Diogenes

Student of War

A prudent man or woman would be wise to educate themselves on the basic strategic patterns and principles of warfare. All the guns, ammo, and supplies will do you absolutely no good if you are not a student of war. Without understanding the complexities of warfare, all your "preps" are in danger of being taken by someone who does understand. You'll be just stocking up "stuff" for somebody else.

"To be prepared for war is one of the most effective means of preserving peace."
— George Washington

The hard truth of our species is that, for centuries, mankind has found it much easier to ruthlessly use savage force to take what he wants rather than to work for it. You can just take one look at the bloody history of mankind to see countless examples of one tribe attacking another to take their women, weapons, land, and food. The "HAVE NOTS" always, eventually, rise up and raid the "HAVES" and take their stuff. Usually killing all the males and taking the women as slaves, in the process.

"In war, the strong make slaves of the weak, and in peace the rich make slaves of the poor."
― *Oscar Wilde*

The Rise of a Leader

In a long term, grid-down environment, I believe there will be ambitious, enterprising, young, bold and savage individuals who have a certain type of charisma. I'm speaking of that kind of religious-cult-leader, magnetic charisma that gets people to follow and to obey every command.

I know there are scores of people who are hoping and praying for an apocalyptic event that brings society into the middle ages again. I've spoken with young men in their early twenties who feel society has not dealt them their fair share of the pie and are very angry. These young men are attracted to violence and power. They are ripe to become true believers in a leader who gives them permission to take what they want. This greatly concerns me, because if that charismatic person leans towards the evil side of the spectrum and provides security and food for followers, a whole lot of innocent people are going to suffer.

If this seems farfetched to some people, I would ask them to consult some recent history. You would have to look no further back than February 25th of 2013 to see the charismatic, Nation of Islam Minister, Louis Farrakhan, giving a controversial speech to roughly 10,000 people. During Farrakhan's speech, he called upon the Chicago city's gang-bangers to serve a better purpose by training to become soldiers who protect his group's assets. He stated that since gang members are "natural soldiers," they could be instructed in "the science of war" and taught to protect the Nation of Islam's property and assets.

The "Occupy Wall Street" movement showed the world that the streets could fill with disenchanted youth in a short period of time. Imagine that times 10,000 or more and throw in all the gang members and 2 million prisoners released from state and federal prisons.

"When one with honeyed words but evil mind persuades the mob, great woes befall the state."
— *Euripides, Orestes*

Know your enemy

"Know your enemy and know yourself; in a hundred battles, you will never be defeated. When you are ignorant of the enemy but know yourself, your chances of winning or losing are equal. If ignorant both of your enemy and of yourself, you are sure to be defeated in every battle."
— *Sun Tzu*

The S.H.T.F. Art of War

Let's take a look at what I believe are the necessary requirements for being a Post-Apocalyptic Criminal Warlord. This will give you an insight as to what sort of enemy you'll be encountering. Understanding that enemy is the first step to defending against that enemy.

Below I've listed the 21 traits and skills I think a Charismatic Apocalyptic Criminal Warlord Leader will possess.

1.Physically Tough

During a SHTF (SHIT HITS THE FAN) apocalyptic event, things will be flat out ruthless and society will have reverted back to savage, tribal politics—meaning only the strongest survive. He'll have to be quick or dead...literally. He's going to have to be in incredible physical shape along with being tough as nails. I'm talking MMA fighter, rodeo bull riding, prison inmate, junk-yard-dog tough.

2. Mean & Nasty

He can absolutely not show any signs of fear or weakness. He cannot afford to have any pity, mercy or remorse. These traits will be a pre-requisite for gaining power and being the leader of a Post-Apocalyptic gang of criminals. He will have what it takes to shoot unarmed people and watch others murder and rape.

Jeffrey M. Olson

"You know how I stayed alive this long? All these years? Fear. The spectacle of fearsome acts. Somebody steals from me, I cut off his hands. He offends me, I cut out his tongue. He rises against me, I cut off his head, stick it on a pike, raise it high up so all on the streets can see. That's what preserves the order of things. Fear."
— Bill "The Butcher" Cutting, Gangs of New York (2002)

3. Bad Reputation

He'll understand how important a killer reputation will be. Fear is a powerful weapon. Going on the war path will deplete valuable ammunition resources and put his troops in harm's way. Medical attention in this fallen world will be primitive at best. Even the slightest injury may lead to infection and death.

To avoid unnecessary fighting and endangering his resources, he'll adopt the tactic of psychological warfare. To strike terror in the hearts and minds of people in the path of his marauders, he'll have to commit unspeakable acts.

He'll use the centuries-old tactic of butchering all the inhabitants of a town and burning it to the ground. That will set a powerful example to all other towns in the area. Once the rumor of these atrocities spreads, the people will surrender instead of fight.

The S.H.T.F. Art of War

"The greatest happiness is to vanquish your enemies, to chase them before you, to rob them of their wealth, to see those dear to them bathed in tears, to clasp to your bosom their wives and daughters."
— Genghis Khan

4. Enhanced Interrogations

Torture will have to be something he is comfortable with. The capture and torture of individuals to gain valuable, tactical information of a stronghold or a plunder-rich area will be necessary to his group's survival.

5. Student of Basic Warfare

The leader of an armed band of marauders will have to have the knowledge to plan and execute a battle plan. Raiding towns and villages will take some understanding of military tactics. He will need to know how to Command and Maneuver troops to take advantage of terrain. He'll have to know how to send out scouts, probe the enemy defenses, infiltrate and capture prisoners. He'll have to know when and when not to fight. He'll have to be confident his troops will know what to do if they're attacked by a rival criminal gang.

Jeffrey M. Olson

6. The Strategies of War

He will have to be able to use the principles of war to navigate the post apocalyptic social and political landscape of this new reality. He'll have to know how to make allies and keep supply lines open. He will have to be able to grasp an overall picture of the battle field.

7. Intelligence Gathering

An above average apocalyptic leader will have radio communication with his gang of thugs. He will also make use of radio scanning devices to listen in on all the radio traffic going on in his area of operation. Advanced knowledge is power. Knowing what is going on, where the authorities are and who's got what and where will be valuable information. During a disaster, the airwaves will be filled with radio chatter.

He won't just use electronic information gathering sources. He'll use human intelligence sources also. In this environment starving, desperate people will spy and give up their neighbors for food or to be spared the agony of watching their children tied to a tree and skinned alive.

8. Nomadic Life Style

He'll have to be on the move constantly. Stay in one place too long and he'll be easier to find and attack. It will make sense to adopt a nomadic lifestyle like the Vikings and Mongol warriors.

9. Soft Targets

Denial will be the first emotion that most people will be experiencing if the current societal structure collapses. Regular, hard working people will not be able to comprehend that the societal structure they've lived in for so long, simply no longer exists. They'll be slow in the realization of their vulnerability. Lack of leadership and bickering will further confuse and paralyze efforts of communities to band together for security. A wise leader of an outlaw band of apocalyptic savages will take advantage of this denial phase of a societal collapse. He will descend on the following places using violence, speed, and surprise:

Churches, Community Centers, Schools, and Charity Organizations – These facilities will more than likely not be defended right away. In times of trouble, these locations will be where the people gather for food and comfort. This is where people and food are going to be for the taking.

100 mile traffic jams – In recent history, millions have fled their homes to avoid the impending doom of a hurricane. People fleeing the cities have been caught up and stranded for days in traffic jams over 100 miles long. These long, unprotected stretches of cash-carrying men, women and children fleeing their homes with their most valuable possessions will be easy pickings. A cunning bandit might even create his own road block or check point to bottleneck the traffic fleeing the cities. The unprepared masses will either run or look the other way if an organized group of armed men begin raping and pillaging their way through this target-rich environment.

Rural Communities - With gun bans and ammo shortages, the weapons of war will be in short supply. The gun stores will have been sold out or looted within 24 hours.

The only place to get weapons, ammo, and supplies will be the private residences. The leader of the criminal hoard will have to overwhelm the stand alone farms and small rural family homes to take their goods. The major population areas are where the biggest trouble will be centered and where the police and military will concentrate their forces. These rural locations will be spread out, on their own and lightly defended.

Suburbs – Just like rural communities, these locations will be where the goods needed for continued survival will be located. They'll literally be the bread and butter of the criminal element.

Lake homes – Usually owned by the elderly and wealthy, these tightly populated, plunder-rich residences literally have their backs against the water and nowhere to run. A well planned attack on these homes will be well worth the effort for a well armed band of marauders. During a societal collapse, these lake homes will be filled with refugees from the surrounding cities; complete

The S.H.T.F. Art of War

with the valuables and supplies they've brought with them.

Hotels and Motels – These will be tidal pools, filled with refugees. They will be easy targets found alongside the plunder-rich, 100 mile traffic jams surrounding large population centers. They will be packed to the limit with refugees carrying their most valuable possessions with them.

10. Inner Circle

A warlord is also going to have to surround himself with a loyal group of equally ruthless captains to make sure his orders get carried out. He'll make use of men of intelligence, skillful in war and natural leaders.

11. Body Guards

Like all men of power, a tough apocalyptic leader will need a personal bodyguard team. The body guards will have to watch out for one of the leader's trusted, inner circle secretly plotting and looking for the right time to take him out, pick up his assault rifle and take over as leader of the group. There will always be someone who thinks he's stronger and smarter than the leader. There will be constant challenges to his authority 24/7. Even with his body guards, he will always have to be watching his back, keeping his gun cocked and sleeping with one eye open.

12. The Complaint Department

Even today, in the pre-SHTF (SHIT HITS THE FAN), comfortable society we live in right now, there's really never a shortage of people complaining about their job, boss or management. Just about everybody has an idea of how they can do a better job than their supervisor or how management sucks and doesn't know what they're doing.

In a SHTF, apocalyptic world…this "management sucks" attitude will be 10 times worse and 10 times deadlier. When people are hungry they become irritable, irrational and their tempers get very short. A brutal leader of a criminal tribe will have to watch his apocalyptic suggestion box with his guns drawn.

13. Spoils of War

This warlord will understand he needs to keep his savage troops loyal. Most of the ancient armies of the past paid their soldiers very little and some did not pay at all. The young men joined up in the fight for what they could acquire from the spoils of war. War looting by victorious armies has been a common practice throughout recorded history. To keep his troops loyal, he'll reward those who have earned merit with the plunder from raids. He'll also ensure his front line troops have the best weapons and equipment.

14. Take a Chill Pill

A leader will be able to handle lots of stress. Making sure his group has water, food, shelter and medical supplies will be just the tip of the iceberg. There will be no days off. His band of cutthroats will look to him for leadership constantly. His ability to manage stress will be unmatched.

15. Bad Apples

Being the leader of an outlaw apocalyptic survival group, he will choose his "people" from the dregs of society. His people will be the criminals who have no love for their fellow man. The outlaw band will be full of killers, rapists, child molesters and other criminal minded scumbags. They will be selfish, violent and brutally sadistic. The applicants for membership will include the mental midgets, wanna-be tough guys and wacked out survivalists. Real, live criminals and scumbags will be flocking to join the group. They will all have mental issues, bad hygiene and an extremely unhealthy problem with authority. To put it mildly, they won't be the best and brightest.

16. Maintaining Order among the disorderly

The warlord will also have to act as the judge to settle disputes and conflicts within the group to maintain order. This will have to be done swiftly and with an iron hand. Death will have to be the sentence to those who challenge his authority.

Jeffrey M. Olson

Whatever decision he may make, he won't be able to make everyone happy. He will be sure to make new enemies with every decision.

His enemies will, assuredly, harbor a grudge against him. Since we're living in a post-apocalyptic scenario, without the rule of law…there'll be nothing to stop that mentally defective, criminally insane person with a grudge, from coming back later and ending the leader's life. I suspect this is usually done from a distance or when his back is turned and he least expects it.

17. Too many mouths to feed

There's strength in numbers but he'll have to watch out and be mindful of how big his band of marauders becomes. More troops will mean more mouths to feed. With more mouths to feed, a leader will have to step up his looting activity to keep his army fat and happy. His troops, like all other soldiers throughout history, will need food, water, boots, clothing, weapons, ammunition and medical attention; not to mention distractions of the female persuasion.

Speaking of the female persuasion, don't assume I think all Post-Apocalyptic warlords have to be males.

18. Post Apocalyptic Commerce

There won't be just one super tough apocalyptic warlord looting, pillaging and slaughtering the surrounding towns and rural areas. There will be competition. An enterprising warlord will see the importance of building alliances.

He will have the forethought to see the eventual need for doing some trading, bargaining and bribing with other savage cutthroat gangs. Slaves, especially women, will be in high demand and of trade value as well as tobacco, cigarettes, medications, booze and narcotics.

19. Post Apocalyptic Romance

Ever hear that old saying that behind every accomplished man is a good woman? Well, if you look at history you'll also find that many a woman behind a great man was also the demise of him. Women throughout history have sold out their man to his enemies for personal gain. They've also simply just killed him off by poisoning him. Even in recent years you can see military generals and politicians having to step down from office or resign because of some indiscretions involving a woman.

" Heaven has no rage like love to hatred turned / Nor hell a fury like a woman scorned."
— William Congreve

So to ensure his longevity, the apocalyptic warlord needs to make his romantic life post-apocalyptically adjusted. A woman he's romantically attached to will be a deadly liability for him and should be avoided at all costs. She will be a weakness his enemies can, and will, use as leverage against him and as bait to lure him into a trap. He's better off having a life philosophy like Robert DeNiro's character *Neil McCauley* in the movie Heat:

"Do not have any attachments, do not have anything in your life you are not willing to walk out on in 30 seconds flat if you spot the heat around the corner."

Women are not to be underestimated. I think it's a mistake to call them the weaker sex. Some women have harnessed their womanly charms and honed their seductive skills to expert precision. Many an emperor has fallen prey and lost his empire to the spells of women such as this. An Apocalyptic Warlord will be cautious and exercise great restraint to ensure he enjoys the charms of the fairer sex but does not fall victim to them.

20. Elusive

He'll fear getting caught. For his own survival, he'll steer clear of any honest law enforcement, military troops or government authority. He will only engage in actions that benefit him and his band of outlaws. Those with bigger guns, more bullets and manpower will be avoided completely.

21. Betrayer

His psychological makeup is one of a professional psychopath. He has no remorse, feelings of guilt or loyalty. His pathological ability to lie is as natural as breathing. He's charismatic, cunning and manipulative. He'll vanish before he's cornered and captured. He will abandon his allegiance to his gang of marauders if he needs to. He'll let them die without a second thought.

When the recovery phase of the societal collapse begins, the new government entity will make the big push to rebuild and get the country back on its feet. They will be out in full force to "pacify" the bandits and criminal warlords. The bandits will be labeled as domestic terrorists, enemies of the state and sovereign criminals. The government will eventually hunt down and dispatch the bad guys with extreme prejudice. They will liberate their weapons, ammo, food and other supplies "for their cause."

History shows that some bad guys betray their gang members and turn them in for a profit. They then enlist with the new government and use their insider bad guy knowledge to help hunt down other criminal gangs for a profit and/or immunity from prosecution.

If you're contemplating the idea of being in a management position at the head of a band of outlaw survivalists during a SHTF situation, I think these examples of the responsibilities and other pitfalls I've listed will make you think twice about it.

What can you do to defend yourself from these marauders?

There are four ways to put forth some type of defense against apocalyptic marauders.

1. The first and most important way is to be in a community or group that is capable of living and working together. Your neighbors will be your life line. The lone-wolf mentality will get you dead the fastest.

2. The second defense is to remain hidden from the bad guys. If you're out of sight you're out of mind. Have a hideout that keeps your daily activity hidden from view.

3. If your location can't be hidden, it should look as unappealing as possible. That's the third method of defense. Your location should appear to have no value whatsoever for even the vilest of the marauding scum.

4. The forth and best defense is to actually have an extremely secure and formidable location. Your community of survivors should turn your location into a very nasty area to attack. The surrounding area to your fortress should have dangers around every rock and tree. Your fortress should

The S.H.T.F. Art of War

make your enemies want to avoid you and move on to other, easier targets.

Post Apocalyptic Side Arm

In the world where there has been a complete SHTF break down of society, I believe it would be wise of you to have the means to defend yourself and your family. That's just common sense.

Firearms and knives are hotly debated topics among the guns-and-gear culture. I see way too many people emotionally attached to their firearm of choice. Firearms are just tools in our survival tool box. A survival weapon is the weapon you have with you when you find yourself in a survival situation. When you're in a fight for your life, you won't care what caliber of lead is being shot in your direction or what the make and model of the weapon that fired it is.

However, having said that, I think a post apocalyptic survivor would do well to have the Ruger Blackhawk, single action, convertible .357/9mm in his inventory.

I'm not "infringing" on a person's right to buy whatever or how-many ever high-priced, legal, firearm/s they want. I'm just saying you might want to consider my recommendation if you can only afford one gun. After all, the single action revolver was the gun that won the west.

Jeffrey M. Olson

I know we live in a modern world where the light weight, semi-auto, high capacity magazine, polymer-frame style guns rule the day. I agree that a high capacity semi-auto handgun would be better suited for combat in the civilized world we currently live in. There's currently a buffet of weapon accessories and lots of ammo available. However, this discussion is focusing on a stark, apocalyptic landscape where there are no gun stores to buy guns and ammo.

The world is changing and we need to change our minds on how we view the future. Gun laws currently—and will continue in the foreseeable future to—make it more difficult to obtain high capacity magazines and firearms that use them. Panic buying as a result of the gun legislation talk by politicians has left gun store shelves empty.

Ammunition costs will be going up and the scarcity of ammunition will cause shooters to shoot less. People are already hording ammunition. In an apocalyptic world with ammunition being extremely scarce, I want to and must get more "bang" for my buck. In a world where scavenging and bartering is the new economy, I'll have to make every round count.

A firearm like the Ruger convertible revolver that can shoot 3 different types of ammunition will have its advantages. Being able to shoot 38 special and 357 magnum is wonderful. Having that extra

The S.H.T.F. Art of War

cylinder to shoot the popular 9mm Luger cartridge out of the same gun is a huge bonus!

They do have their drawbacks. They only hold six rounds and are slow to load and heavy. However, revolvers are simpler, rugged and debatably more reliable than semi-autos. They are not finicky about the ammo they shoot. Malfunctions like "stove pipe," "failure to feed" and "double feed" are not something an individual with a revolver will have to worry about.

Studies show that most gunfights happen at close range and only a few rounds are fired. I'm sure there are exceptions to this study finding. However, I think the potential for someone engaging multiple attackers for a long period of time is unrealistic. If you're being attacked by multiple assailants, the odds are against you. You're going to be dead before you can pull your pistol. Very few people train enough on a daily basis to even come close to having the tactical edge to win a gunfight against one person, let alone two or more. If someone gets the drop on you, you're at their mercy. They'll shoot you in the back and take your boots, guns and gear. Ambushing an adversary is the standard post-apocalyptic operating procedure if you want to win with minimal injury to yourself.

At this writing, these convertible revolvers are becoming extremely hard to come by. As more and more preparedness-minded people come to realize the advantage of having this "old school" weapon in their inventory, it will become almost impossible to get.

The Main Battle Rifle

If you have a choice between a rifle and a handgun, I'd recommend the rifle. I've heard it said that *"The only purpose for a pistol is to fight your way back to the rifle you should never have laid down."*

On that note, I just think it's a complete waste of money buying what most doomsday preppers and survivalists advise.

They tell you that at a minimum you're going to need a Handgun, Military Style AK or AR-15 Main Battle rifle, Sniper rifle, 12 gauge Shotgun and 22 caliber rifle; not to mention the 2,000 rounds you need for each weapon. That's simply ridiculous and too expensive for most people. The current political atmosphere of gun control legislation is making it extremely difficult to find some of these "prepper recommended" weapons and all the accessories for them.

You can save up for a regular old 22 rifle by putting your pocket change in a jar everyday for a few months or sell some of your kids old video games on eBay. Plus you can get 500 rounds of 22 ammunition for under $30. It doesn't take a rocket scientist to see the logic in this.

The S.H.T.F. Art of War

I just don't see the practicality of having all those prepper recommended guns and all that ammo when you can only hold one gun at a time. If it's a SHTF, post-apocalyptic, lawless land you're living in…all the bad guys have to do is surround you and pick you off from a distance. Look up siege warfare and see how effective that was throughout history. It won't be a stand-up fair fight where the good guys always win. You'll be out picking tomatoes in your survival garden or chopping wood when you get sniped by some punk with a scoped rifle. All those guns won't help you at all.

"Sometimes you have to pick the gun up to put the Gun down."
— Malcolm X

The Flow of Crime

Water seeks the path of least resistance. So do criminals. Criminals for the most part are cowards and attack the easiest targets. They may be lazy but they aren't dumb about self-protection. They, too, will realize that there's an absence of hospitals and quality medical care. They won't want to receive any bullet holes or injuries that will cause them to miss out on all the pillaging and raping that's going on.

"The choice is not between violence and nonviolence but between nonviolence and nonexistence."
— Martin Luther King Jr.

Jeffrey M. Olson

During hurricane Katrina, homeowners would fire off a round or two in the air when they saw gangs of "would-be" looters coming down their street at night. This effectively encouraged them to move on to other "gun-free" neighborhoods.

"Violence, naked force, has settled more disputes in history than has any other factor and the contrary opinion is wishful thinking at its worst. Breeds that forget this basic truth have always paid for it with their lives and freedoms."
— *Robert Heinlein*

The S.H.T.F. Art of War

Part 2
How to be a FEMA Camp Hero

This is probably the most controversial chapter of my entire book. So buckle up!

Keep these points in mind as you read:

1. The following information is for people who have become displaced and have *no other choice* but to seek refuge at a FEMA disaster recovery center.

2. Never say never! Even the most hardcore preppers/survivalists may find themselves in a situation with no other choice than to seek assistance from FEMA.

3. A major part of survival, after all, is being prepared for the things we wish to avoid.

4. I say again, millions of people WILL have NO OTHER CHOICE but to seek out help at a FEMA recovery center.

5. I've done my research on FEMA's history and hope never to be in a FEMA Camp. However, if unfortunate events befall me and I find myself in one, I'm glad to have the knowledge I've shared here in this

book, to help me get through the ordeal intact.

6. I differ with a lot of preppers on the FEMA concentration camp topic. I don't believe these FEMA centers are concentration camps built to exterminate people as some conspiracy theorists propose.

7. I believe you can take "some" comfort in knowing that a government cannot exist without people to govern! They need us. Well, at least most of us.

8. The government, power elites and the super rich need a labor force to do the dirty work. The rich and powerful don't get their hands dirty. Their biggest fear is the loss of their vast fortunes.

9. Their top priority will be to protect their assets and the continuity of the lavish lifestyle they are accustomed to. Those with great power will do whatever is necessary to ensure they keep that power. Would it not make sense that those power elites have a plan in place to keep the status quo?

10. I don't know what that plan is, but I'm pretty sure it isn't the wholesale extermination of United States citizens.

The S.H.T.F. Art of War

I've said I don't think FEMA camps are WW2-era Nazi concentration camps. However, I'll be the first to say that Internment camps for political dissidents in the U.S. aren't a conspiracy theory. The Department of Defense has a document entitled "Internment and Relocation Operations" or FM 3-39.40. Created in 2010 and predating the N.D.A.A (National Defense Authorization Act) of 2012. The U.S. ARMY even advertises for the **INTERNMENT/RESETTLEMENT SPECIALIST (31E)** job position on its recruiting web site under careers and jobs.

"In the strict sense of the term, a true democracy has never existed, and never will exist. It is against natural order that the great number should govern and that the few should be governed. -Jean-Jacques Rousseau.

Inalienable Rights

The traditional American philosophy teaches that man, the individual, is endowed at birth with rights which are inalienable because they're given by his creator. Inalienable rights are by definition non-negotiable, God-given rights—incapable of being alienated, surrendered or transferred; received at birth, from God and enduring as natural law itself.

WARNING! I have no desire to offend anyone of faith. However, the following may sting a bit to the devoutly religious. Logic, facts and reason seem to always have a way of clashing with religion. I recognize and respect the difference between

Jeffrey M. Olson

organized-group religion and personal spiritual foundation.

1. This author believes in the freedom from religion as well as freedom of religion.

2. I'm not a very big fan of books, religions or belief systems that instruct their followers to slaughter those who do not believe as they do.

3. People who claim an invisible deity has sanctioned the murder of other tribes or innocent civilians in the past and in the present, scare me.

4. I fear religions and people who spread their "message" through fear and suppress new knowledge about the universe we live in.

My personal view of religion can be best described by what astronaut Gene Cernan said after making the last moon-landing in 1972.

"I felt that the world was just too beautiful to have happened by accident. There has to be something bigger than you and bigger than me, and I mean this in a spiritual sense, not a religious sense. There has to be a creator of the universe who stands above the religions that we ourselves create to govern our lives."

With that being said, I believe your civil rights are not given by a creator or grand designer of the universe. I like those inalienable rights just as much as you. But it was man who developed those rights and it is man who can and does change them and take them away. If you are a person of faith and reading this book, you can save your hate mail. I know I cannot change some people's minds about their religious beliefs and won't attempt to try. I think debate on any issue is a good thing. Debating issues and philosophies is healthy. It allows new ideas to enter into the mix. However, religion is different. Religions today seem stagnant and are not going to come up with any new arguments unless they start to tolerate some new perspectives.

If you question someone's religion they get emotionally charged and upset and accuse you of being rude, aggressive and intolerant. Many religions have contrived to make it impossible to disagree with them critically without being rude. Anything these days can be questioned, but religion is often held off the table of rational criticism.

Physicists aren't offended when their view of physics is disproved or challenged. And yet there's a kind of tribal, and ultimately dangerous, reflexive response to having most mainstream religious ideas challenged.

Jeffrey M. Olson

If I could avoid suggesting a religious dialog in this book I would. However, since I'm covering the topic of God-given "inalienable rights," I can't avoid the religious aspect attached to those rights. I wish more people of faith would adopt and practice this quote from one of our founding fathers:

"I never considered a difference of opinion in politics, in religion, in philosophy, as cause for withdrawing from a friend."
-Thomas Jefferson

People can and will still believe that an invisible supreme being gave them those inalienable rights. However, the hard, honest truth is, it's the man/men in power that allow/s you to exercise those rights. A quick fact check of all the wars and ethnic cleansing that have been done throughout mankind's bloody history proves this point. For whatever reason, a supreme being hasn't seen a need to jump in and stop these atrocities yet.

During a national emergency, a nationwide, SHTF (shit hits the fan) event that doomsday preppers fear, *our Government* would implement Martial Law. *Our Government* would suspend the constitution and those God-given, "Inalienable rights." This includes the right to bear arms, as was seen with gun confiscations during hurricane Katrina in 2005.

"Laws are silent in times of war."
— *Marcus Tullius Cicero*

The S.H.T.F. Art of War

You must remember that a *Governmental system*, like with most living systems, will do whatever is necessary to protect and preserve itself when threatened with extinction.

Martial Law

Martial Law is the imposition of military rule by military authorities over designated regions on an emergency basis—(usually) only temporary— when the civilian government or civilian authorities fail to function effectively (e.g., maintain order and security, and provide essential services), when there are extensive riots and protests, or when the disobedience of the law becomes widespread. In most cases, military forces are deployed to quiet the crowds, to secure government buildings and key or sensitive locations, and to maintain order. Generally, military personnel replace civil authorities and perform some or all of their functions. In full-scale martial law, the highest-ranking military officer would take over, or be installed, as the military governor or as head of the government, thus removing all power from the previous executive, legislative, and judicial branches of government.

The United States already has a plan for the continuity of government and rule of law during an SHTF event. I say that's a good thing. I like that my government has a "prepper" mindset. I always find it strange that doomsday preppers and survivalists are shocked and surprised that their government has a plan to survive in the case of a nationwide or worldwide emergency.

Would you feel safer if they didn't?

With that being said, I also think you shouldn't depend on the *U.S. Government* to be at your doorstep within 24 hours of an emergency with a blanket and box of food for you. When a crisis happens, it's no secret they expect some of us not to survive. They also expect a great many of us to at least pick ourselves up, dust off the dirt and mud and press on. Be mindful of the fact that the U.S. Government does not have a stellar track record on responding to natural disaster emergencies. A country-wide emergency will severely test the limits of its recovery effectiveness.

It's a safe bet to say you'll be on your own for a very long time. And even a short time will seem like a very long time, when disaster has struck. It would be a good time to get to know your neighbors—before a disaster strikes.

I'll be the first to admit we don't have a perfect government. However, I believe it's a better system to have in place right now than any other. Like it or hate it, the U.S. government is very powerful and does have executive orders in place to ensure its continuity and keep the rule of law. I for one believe that, as citizens of this country, we

The S.H.T.F. Art of War

should support and do what we can to help our community and the country survive and get back on its feet if/when a major disaster ever happens.

Here's a list and brief description of some of those executive orders.

"The only way to make a difference is to acquire power."
— Hilary Rodham Clinton

Executive Order List

EXECUTIVE ORDER 10990

Allows the government to take over all modes of transportation and control of highways and sea ports.

EXECUTIVE ORDER 10995

Allows the government to seize and control the communication media.

EXECUTIVE ORDER 10997

Allows the government to take over all electrical power, gas, petroleum, fuels and minerals.

Jeffrey M. Olson

EXECUTIVE ORDER 10998

Allows the government to seize all means of transportation, including personal cars, trucks or vehicles of any kind and take total control over all highways, sea ports and waterways.

EXECUTIVE ORDER 10999

Allows the government to take over all food resources and farms.

EXECUTIVE ORDER 11000

Allows the government to mobilize civilians into work brigades under government supervision.

EXECUTIVE ORDER 11001

Allows the government to take over all health, education and welfare functions.

EXECUTIVE ORDER 11002

Designates the Postmaster General to operate a national registration of all persons.

EXECUTIVE ORDER 11003

Allows the government to take over all airports and aircraft, including commercial aircraft.

EXECUTIVE ORDER 11004

Allows the Housing and Finance Authority to relocate communities, build new housing with public funds, designate areas to be abandoned and establish new locations for populations.

EXECUTIVE ORDER 11005

Allows the government to take over railroads, inland waterways and public storage facilities.

EXECUTIVE ORDER 11051

Specifies the responsibility of the Office of Emergency Planning and gives authorization to put all Executive Orders into effect in times of increased international tensions and economic or financial crisis.

EXECUTIVE ORDER 11310

Grants authority to the Department of Justice to enforce the plans set out in Executive Orders, to institute industrial support, to establish judicial and legislative liaison, to control all aliens, to operate penal and correctional institutions and to advise and assist the President.

Jeffrey M. Olson

EXECUTIVE ORDER 11921

Allows the Federal Emergency Preparedness Agency (FEMA) to develop plans to establish control over the mechanisms of production and distribution, of energy sources, wages, salaries, credit and the flow of money in U.S. financial institutions in any undefined national emergency. It also provides that when a state of emergency is declared by the President, Congress cannot review the action for six months.

The Federal Emergency Management Agency has broad powers in every aspect of the nation. General Frank Salzedo, chief of FEMA's Civil Security Division stated in a 1983 conference that he saw FEMA's role as a "new frontier in the protection of individual and governmental leaders from assassination, and of civil and military installations from sabotage and/or attack, as well as prevention of dissident groups from gaining access to U.S. opinion, or a global audience in times of crisis." FEMA's powers were consolidated by President Carter to incorporate the.... National Security Act of 1947 allows for the strategic relocation of industries, services, government and other essential economic activities, and to rationalize the requirements for manpower, resources and production facilities.

To make it clear to all the Doomsday Preppers and Survivalists who have bug out vehicles and bug out bags, for those citizens who have stockpiles of food weapons and ammo: Everything, I mean absolutely *everything* you have, to include your gold and silver, can be confiscated by government authorities and used for the greater good to rebuild this country. During a societal collapse, you and all your stuff belongs to Uncle Sam and subsequently can possibly be divvied up to the unprepared individuals in the FEMA camps.

I will also add this: Martial Law is only supposed to be put in place as a temporary measure until the crisis has passed. However, in a major societal collapse that doomsday preppers fear, martial law could last for *decades* and the constitutional rights that get suspended during a declaration of martial law may never come back. I suspect a new liberal, socialistic constitution will be drafted up, that only vaguely resembles the old one.

Pick a winning SHTF survival team

You have to keep in mind that human nature hasn't changed at all throughout history.

Societies have always run on these rules:

1. *The strongest get what they want before the weakest.*
2. *Men have always subjugated other men in one fashion or another.*

3. The people with the money and wealth make the rules.
4. The people who have weapons enforce the rules.

We humans are a tribal species. Our chances of survival are better if we are in a group. The big question must be: which group to align ourselves with during a complete collapse of the country as we know it?

You will have 3 main groups to choose from.

Group #1
I'll call group #1 the **Good Guys**. They consist of a local community of fair minded, ethical people, who band together and help each other during the turbulent time of a great crisis.

Group #2
I'll call group #2 the **Bad Guys**. As told in chapter 1, these marauder groups and types will be operational almost immediately. Based on historical fact, they will be on scene way before any FEMA outreach program can be of assistance to the desperate, hapless, woefully unprepared populace. These bad guy groups will be gaining in numbers and mobilizing alarmingly fast.

They will accomplish this by using methods and tactics that have been proven to be highly successful throughout history. They will be looting, pillaging, raping and torturing to get more

The S.H.T.F. Art of War

guns, food and supplies. I predict group #2 will initially have the advantage over group #1 because group #1 will be unprepared and take much longer to get organized. Group #1 will also have those inconvenient road blocks like moral consciousness and good will towards their fellow man to deal with.

Group #3
FEMA, although very slow to respond, will have the United States Military with all its manpower, night vision technology, guns, armor, tanks, artillery, air power, unmanned drones and other support services. They will have vast supplies of food, and field medical facilities.

I'm fully aware that the organization with the acronym FEMA strikes fear into the heart of many a survivalist. I suspect there are people right now gasping in disgust that I am even mentioning FEMA as an option for their survival.

In the big picture of life-and-death survival, it really doesn't matter if you are pro-FEMA or anti-FEMA. The organization is a reality and to MILLIONS of survivors who've lost everything, FEMA will be their ONLY option and sound like the winning team to join up with.

<u>**Asset or Liability**</u>
If you find yourself in a desperate position where you have to choose group 1 or 2 to align your

loyalties with for survival.... You should be honest with yourself and ask yourself...are you a leader or a follower? It's a very important question. It's perfectly ok to not be a leader. There's no shame in that at all. In fact, even if you do have leadership qualities, it may be in your best interest to not step up and be in a leadership role during these dangerous times.

I think it's a good strategy to just play a support role to the Alpha Male in your survival group. The person in charge will have tremendous amounts of stress placed upon him. He will be responsible for the short and long term survival of the group. For now you'll need to work on securing your place within the group. Having some kind of medical, technical, mechanical or other practical skill will go further than being a lawyer, banker or salesman.

The leader will look upon you, judging whether you are an asset or liability to the group. He'll have to consider whether or not you're worth the precious food and water it will take to keep you within the group. The leader will more than likely assign a value to you. Increasing your value to the group also increases your overall survivability within the group.

You goal is **not** to be on the expendable list.

The S.H.T.F. Art of War

Is FEMA Right For You?

If you have no real worth to a post-apocalyptic survival group and feel you'd be put immediately on the survival group's expendable list, then you should consider getting your worthless butt to a FEMA camp as soon as possible, so to speak.

Now...I'm all for self sufficiency and being "Off Grid" as much as possible. I believe you should be supplementing your food supply with a garden. I'm also in favor of having a small stock pile of long term food for unexpected disasters and emergencies.

During an all out nationwide disaster or infrastructure collapse, having a stash of food and supplies ahead of time will only last so long. Like I said, you don't have to like it, but FEMA will be coming. It's an unrealistic fantasy to think you or your survival group can hold out forever without contact from another hostile group or new government trying to rebuild the country.

I've received a lot of hate mail on this subject. It still doesn't change the fact that it's inevitable for your preparations to run out or be taken by forces stronger than yours. It's also highly possible that your stash, if found, may also be "liberated" by FEMA for the common good of everybody.

At this point I must tell you again that I'm neither pro- or anti-FEMA. I'm a survivor and will consider

Jeffrey M. Olson

all options to stay alive if I find myself in a worst-case situation of a complete societal collapse.

There are a lot of preppers and survivalists who think the government will just disappear in the event of a societal collapse. That's just not going to happen. Even if it does, a new one will be implemented eventually. I would also caution those who wish for another civil war in America. If the Federal Government ever loses its control during a societal collapse, a civil war with **multiple** factions will ensue. These diametrically opposed, uncompromising factions will struggle to gain control and impose their idea of how to rebuild.

In this scenario, once America collapses, it won't be coming back to its former self. What will emerge will be new countries with new borders. When Rome collapsed it re-emerged as France, Spain and Italy. Germany and England were also once a part of the Roman Empire. The fall of Rome was also followed by a little thing called "The Dark Ages" which lasted for a few hundred years.

History shows that food shortages and disease immediately follow every societal collapse or civil war. As unappealing as it may be, a very large number of desperate people will consider coming on in for the big win and join the FEMA team during a doomsday apocalypse.

The S.H.T.F. Art of War

I can see the marketing campaign signs now.

"Ask not what your FEMA camp can do for you, but what can YOU do for your FEMA camp."

The Benefits of a FEMA Camp

Let's take a look of the benefits of having to go to a FEMA camp.

Some people are not cut out to be the lonely hero on the road with his trusty rifle and survival bug out bag. This makes for some fun reading but it's not at all realistic. I say a man has got to know his limitations.

Doomsday Preppers and survivalists will tell you that FEMA camps are actually concentration camps to be feared and avoided at all costs. Like I said before, I disagree. I believe that is simply false. It's also worthy to note that the same preppers who preach New World Order conspiracy theories, will most likely be the ones who will kill you for what you have in your bug out bag when they become desperate.

While interviewing young preppers for this book, I found an alarming number of those preppers were all gun and no preps. They had no other plan than to threaten or kill others and take the stuff they need to survive. It's a safe bet that all the paranoid, anti-government preppers will eventually be just as dangerous as criminal gangs and outlaw survivalists when they become desperate. They already look at the unprepared as sheep.

So let's pretend the crap has really hit the fan and the country is in tough shape and getting worse extremely fast.

Let's say you're one of the legions of people who can't afford a year's supply of dehydrated food or a tricked out assault rifle with 2,000 rounds of ammo. You can't raise sheep, rabbits or plant a garden. You know nothing about stacking gold and silver coins and couldn't afford it if you did.

Maybe, just maybe a FEMA camp is just the thing for you.

For one thing, it's a lot cheaper. You don't have to waste your time and money on prepping. You can have a "prepper peace of mind" and enjoy the now, knowing you have a FEMA camp plan in place for a SHTF event. After all, things are really bad and it's a matter of survival at this point. Starvation and disease always follow a major disaster. I should point out that epidemic dysentery is a major problem among refugee populations, where overcrowding and poor sanitation facilitate transmission. Worldwide, approximately 140 million people develop dysentery each year, and about 600,000 die.

The S.H.T.F. Art of War

Even with that sobering statistic, your local FEMA recovery center will be a better place than most during a collapse of society. Not the best mind you, but better than most. Sure you will have to do your part on the work detail. You probably can't come and go as you please...but you'll have 3 meals a day and a cot to sleep on. You'll have a roof over your head and medical attention if need be.

1. Apocalyptic America will be extremely dangerous. At the FEMA camp, you'll be guarded from roving bands of armed, survivalist cutthroats who are pillaging and raping the country side at will.

2. At the FEMA camp you won't have to deal with the drama and medieval politics of trying to fit into an armed, close knit, paranoid, Doomsday prepper, survivalist group.

3. You won't have to worry about guard duty, internal power struggles over leadership or fights over who's getting more rations or who's sleeping with whom.

4. I also suspect those roving gangs of cutthroat bandits will attack other survivalist groups first before they attempt an attack on your well-armed FEMA camp. The FEMA camp will have heavily armed guards

with night vision and unmanned drones overhead.

5. Besides, once the government pacifies the bandits, they will go after those Doomsday Prepper survivalist groups to encourage them to join team FEMA. FEMA and DHL will want them to come on in for the big push to rebuild and get the country back on its feet.

The groups who resist will be labeled as domestic terrorists, enemies of the state, and sovereign criminals. The government will eventually pacify them and liberate their weapons, ammo, food, and other supplies "for the cause".

I propose living at the FEMA camp could possibly be a better option if you have no other choice. The nearest FEMA recovery camp may be the only way to ensure you and your family will have food, shelter and relative safety during the societal collapse.

How to prepare for your FEMA camp stay

If a major disaster or an all out societal collapse ever happens and you choose to or are forced to go to a FEMA recovery center, I find it would be best to be prepared for that scenario. After all, preparing mentally and physically in advance for the unpleasant and unthinkable is the definition of a prepper or survivalist mindset.

The S.H.T.F. Art of War

If you find yourself at a FEMA camp, it would make sense to be the first one at the FEMA camp gates to get the best bunk! In preparation for dealing with massive numbers of unprepared survivors, I figure FEMA camps are modeled like the prison system minus the cell bars. So with this in mind, I have some advice for your FEMA camp stay:

It will be important to have a valid form of identification with you. A driver's license or passport is the most preferred I.D.

Scan Copies of Important Documents like your Driver's license and passport and put them on a flash drive or external hard drive. If you've been in the military service, you should also scan your DD Form 214 along with any special training certificates you may have. Your resume, college transcripts, and any other documents you feel are important should be put on there as well.

Your FEMA Bug out Bag- During an emergency of this apocalyptic magnitude, you'd be smart to pack light. Pack your FEMA Bug out Bag with only the things you'll need at the FEMA recovery camp.

Good quality work boots- are a must. You may be on your feet all day. The combat/duty boot industry is booming with a lot of choices. New, light weight desert style boots dominate the scene. Don't buy cheap boots to put on your feet! Based on personal experience, I prefer the ALTAMA and

Matterhorn brand boots. Don't forget to have extra boot laces.

Safety glasses- have come a long way in style and design from the ones the shop teachers used to wear in the 1970's. Modern safety glasses today have UV protection, distortion free polycarbonate lenses, soft rubber nose pieces, cushioned rubber temple pads, and a multitude of lens colors. Home Depot and Menards type stores are a great place to get quality safety glasses for a fraction of the cost of high end sunglasses. I purchased a 5 pack of safety glasses with tinted lenses for 10 bucks and still use them today. Don't forget to have a case to protect your glasses and a cord that allows the glasses to hang around your neck when not in use.

Hygiene items- such as dental floss, a tooth brush, tooth paste, chap-stick, shaving kit and fingernail clipper.

If you can smuggle an item into the FEMA camp, I'd suggest it be Dr. Bronners Hemp-Peppermint Magic 18-in-1 soap. You can use this soap to shave, brush your teeth, scrub your noggin, and take a bath.

Shower shoes- to avoid foot fungus in the showers.

The S.H.T.F. Art of War

Sewing Kit- Make your own small sewing kit with a variety of medium to large needles, buttons, and heavy duty thread that match the clothes you wear. The pre-made sewing kits you can buy have needles that are too small and thread that breaks too easily.

Extra socks and underwear- This needs no explanation of why. If it does, then a FEMA camp definitely is for you.

Heavy duty work shirts- work pants, and a couple pairs of leather work gloves. Don't forget a leather belt. Food rations might be a little lean and along with all the work…you're going lose a little weight.

The Dentist- They probably won't have the best dental care in the FEMA camp so if you need some dental work, it would be a good idea to get it done now.

Eye glasses- are another important item to make sure you have a few pairs of. Who knows if you'll be able to get another pair in the FEMA camp?

A walking cane- Since weapons of any kind won't be allowed into the FEMA recovery facility, you might want to consider bringing a walking cane. The walking stick and cane are commonplace in many cultures, both as walking aids and historically as defensive implements. Predators prefer to attack the unarmed. A person without a stick is easier to attack than a person with a stick.

Flashlight- An indispensable item during a disaster. I recommend you stay away from flashlights with special batteries. I recommend you get one that uses batteries that are more common and easier to find like a AA battery. Pick a "thumb switch" style flashlight with an aluminum body. If attacked, it can be used as an improvised striking device during an attack.

Barter items- The FEMA disaster recovery camps will be very crowded with hordes of unprepared citizens. An enterprising individual will do very well if they've thought ahead and brought with them extra, high demand items to trade with the other survivors.

Cloth and leather work gloves will be very valuable to the work details.

It may be a long time until the country is up and running again and store shelves are not empty. The scarcity of any hygienic items, like toothpaste & shampoo, will make them valuable and in high demand.

Simple over the counter medications like Aspirin and Ibuprofen will also be in need to help soothe the aches and pains of manual labor. Prescription pain killers will be of the highest value; however,

The S.H.T.F. Art of War

those will be in very short supply and best kept stashed for emergencies only.

Twenty Five Refugee Rules for FEMA Camp Survival

1. Normal Rules No Longer Apply

Above all, remember that the normal rules of society simply don't apply any longer. When you're in the FEMA camp, you're living on a different planet where all that matters to you is surviving the experience with as little damage as possible.

The camp will have rules and regulations so make sure you get a copy of the rules. You can probably be punished for breaking the rules even if you don't know them.

2. Have a positive attitude

You want to impress the guards, FEMA staff, your shift leader and tent supervisor. Show them that you're not a trouble maker and you have no problem putting in a full day's work at 100%.

3. Don't bitch, whine or complain

There is no shortage of negative people to do that. No one wants to be around that type of person. The five minutes you just spent complaining is five minutes you just wasted—and that's the best possible of several potential outcomes.

Jeffrey M. Olson

4. Special Talents, Skills & Certifications

When signing into the FEMA camp, make it known if you posses any special skills such as a welder, nurse, engineer, doctor or heavy equipment operator. Any skills that will aid in the reconstruction of society will be a plus.

5. Find people who come from the same place you do

When you get to your designated FEMA facility, you need to find other survivors who are from your city or state. They will be your hometown gang and they will usually help you with things you have an immediate need for, such as basic hygiene items, shoes, etc.

6. Know every square inch of your operating area

Know which way North is. Have an updated map of the area you'll be operating or living in. Know the location of the police stations, hospitals, military installations, embassies, airport and check points. It's not a bad idea to have your own map.

7. Be a mentor to the new guys

Be the genuine friendly face that welcomes a new survivor and gives them advice on how things work around their new environment. First impressions are everything. This also helps build

The S.H.T.F. Art of War

alliances for the future. Remember: **Network! - Network! - Network!**

8. Know who the power players are

I hate the office politics just as much as the next guy. You don't have to be involved in them, but you at least better understand the dynamics of your workplace pecking order. Know who the power players are.

9. Always keep your eyes and ears open to spot an opportunity

It will be a "selfish" "every-man-for-himself" world in the FEMA camp. The only way to get ahead or get extra anything will be to hustle. Being alert for opportunities will be a full time job.

10. Don't underestimate people

Looks are deceiving. Just because they "talk the talk" and have all the high speed gear doesn't mean they know their stuff. And vice versa, by the way.

11. Don't believe every rumor you hear

Don't repeat or spread rumors. When in doubt go to the source.

12. Don't trust anyone

That goes for guards, other FEMA officials and the person in the room or tent next door. Remember this is an all-out survival situation where society as you know it has collapsed. If someone is being nice to you, ask yourself "What's in it for them?" They almost always have some hidden motive that you don't know about. In a FEMA camp, nothing is free. For example, if someone gives or loans you something, you will probably have to pay it back with a hefty rate of interest added. If you can't pay, they may demand a favor that could get you into big trouble, like hiding contraband, or worse.

13. Emotions are your worst enemy

Emotions reveal your weaknesses. It's possible for other survivors, guards, and FEMA staff to prey on weakness. Don't give them the opportunity to do so. If someone can figure out what makes you angry, they can use that knowledge to manipulate you. In the same way, if someone knows what makes you happy, they can try to ruin it for you. And because the camps will be crowded, privacy will be almost non-existent and many other people will be around you 24/7; they'll have unlimited opportunities to test their manipulative skills on you.

14. Journal

Keep a daily journal of your life while on your FEMA camp adventure. It helps organize your thoughts.

The S.H.T.F. Art of War

15. Do not be overly friendly with your FEMA campmates but do ask some questions

Many survivors may have been at the camp longer than you and will be able to give you information about the camp and the system itself. You will have to judge for yourself whether to believe any of the information or not. Use common sense and try to figure out if that person has a reason to lie or mislead you. Some FEMA campers will try to intimidate new arrivals or mislead them for fun. Be careful.

16. Don't tell people anything they don't need to know

Choose your words carefully. Potentially, anything you say to guards, FEMA staff or other campers (no matter how innocent you think it is) can be used to hurt you, manipulate you or can be taken out of context to get you into trouble. Avoid discussing dangerous conversation topics. Otherwise, it can easily get you into trouble. Obvious subjects to steer clear of are religion, politics, racial issues, or your own personal feelings about someone or their family and friends. Some of the campers you'll encounter may have a short temper, or are mentally ill, of low intelligence or just plain bad. FEMA campers like that don't have a warning written on their foreheads—they look like regular guys and gals. You can easily be misunderstood or deliberately misquoted by someone who's trying to stir up trouble. What starts out as a petty argument over a trivial issue can turn into someone bearing a strong personal grudge against you. Don't be paranoid. Just be aware that things may not be what they seem, e.g., the FEMA camper who tells you that gay or Mexican people are just like everyone else, then asks what you think may in reality hate homosexuals or Mexican people—he's just testing your attitude or yanking your chain.

17. Always be polite and respectful to guards and other FEMA camp employees, even if they are evil SOBs

That's because if you piss them off, they are holding all the cards and can make your life harder than it already is. So, don't give them a stick to beat you with. It's true that some FEMA employees are better than others. Even so, never forget whose side they're on—it certainly isn't yours. You need to get it in your head that the staff is always right and you need to do what they say; even if you know it is wrong at the time, it is best to just follow the order, and if you have a problem with it you can address it at some later point. Example: You work as a server in the kitchen and a staff supervisor tells you to go clean garbage cans in the dining room. You know that is not part of your duties and that you usually do not clean garbage cans, but the best thing to do in this situation is to just go clean the garbage cans, because you are a FEMA camper and you are not

The S.H.T.F. Art of War

going to win an argument with a FEMA staff member. Don't do anything that makes the staff feel challenged or intimidated; they have various ways of making you pay for that mistake. You don't want to be on the "troublemaker" list.

18. Don't get a reputation as a "snitch"

People who tell tales to the guards or other FEMA campers are despised by everyone and can be physically attacked. The best thing you can do in a FEMA camp is to see everything, hear everything and say nothing. If the FEMA guards ask you for information about some incident involving other campers, claim that you were looking the other way and didn't notice or hear anything. While this may irritate the staff—on some level—that you aren't willing to snitch, they will likely understand.

19. Focus on the now

When you enter the FEMA camp, try to concentrate on what's going on inside camp, because it will help you keep your sanity. It's difficult not to think about the things you're missing since the collapse of the outside world, but torturing yourself with that will just make you miserable. It certainly won't get you out of the FEMA camp any faster. Instead, concentrate on the things you can control in the camp, not the things that are out of your reach outside the FEMA fence.

Jeffrey M. Olson

20. Keep a low profile

Try to blend into the background when you are in the FEMA camp. Stay under the radar of guards and other FEMA employees. Basically, don't draw attention to yourself if you can avoid it. Remember that the nail that stands out gets hammered in. Watch and learn.

21. The walls have ears

Bear in mind that anything you say is likely to be overheard by both FEMA campers and guards. There are snitches among your fellow campers, who are looking to trade information for favors with the staff. Be especially careful about criticizing other FEMA campers, as you can pretty much guarantee that it will get back to them.

22. Protect yourself at all times

Hopefully you will never be physically attacked during your time in the FEMA camp. However, if you are, here are some points to bear in mind. You can be attacked anywhere in the camp, though usually it will happen in a place where there is no direct surveillance by guards. Your attackers will know where those surveillance "blind spots" are. Obviously, a classic place for an attack is the toilet or shower, when you are distracted. An attacker can seize a time-window of just 30 seconds to attack you, then walk away nonchalantly. So, watch their hands because

The S.H.T.F. Art of War

that's where the attack comes from. If someone has their hands in their pockets or behind their back, they could be concealing an improvised weapon such as a knife. Don't let yourself get backed into a corner where you have no escape route away from your attacker.

This may sound weird and uncomfortable, but could be life-saving: If you are concerned about getting attacked, sit when you go to the bathroom, and take your pants off completely. In prisons, many attacks happen when you are using the toilet; it's easier to defend yourself without your pants around your ankles, so you won't trip "caught with your pants down," as the saying goes.

23. Constipation

Drink plenty of water. The travel, change of environment, diet and new work routine have the tendency to cause stress on your body and may constipate you.

This can become a serious medical problem. Drinking plenty of water helps combat this phenomenon.

24. Apocalyptic book recommendations

To survive in a post-societal-collapsed world, you're going to have to approach this new life a lot differently. You'll have to kiss that old life of trivial and pointless information that gets you nowhere goodbye. In this new hostile world, I highly believe you should absorb all the information that's more relevant to the environment you're in. Knowledge is power after all. You will be surrounded by a lot of distressed and disturbed citizens if the world has turned upside down. Find some books that help you recognize and deal with toxic people. Survival of the fittest will be the rule of the land. The world will be medieval, so books on the art of war and other warfare strategies will be full of valuable knowledge. Both of these book topics will aid you in navigating this brave new hostile world.

25. Complacency Kills

One of the more difficult aspects of refugee life is staying focused when nothing ever happens. Long hours of boredom and monotony make the mind wander off. The enemy knows this and will use it against you. *Don't get complacent.*

Part 3
<u>SHTF Traffic Sucks.</u>

I hear a lot of preppers and survivalists talking about how people will be fleeing the cities during some type of disaster or SHTF Event.

"A lot of people will be getting out of Dodge and heading for the hills," they say.

The talk never seems to go much further or deeper than that. They seem to never entertain the thought that, despite their best efforts, they themselves might be stranded in the nightmarish scenario of hundreds of miles of grid-locked traffic.

It doesn't matter if it's an EMP, solar flare, earthquake, global financial crash or pandemic that causes a societal collapse. In a major event such as this, everyone in the disaster area will be hitting the road to get out of the city. Multitudes of panicked, urban dwellers will be freaking out and grabbing everything they can as they take to the highways to escape. Millions of refugees will spill out, unprepared, into the countryside of rural America.

In recent years people have fled, by the thousands, to get away from areas of an impending storm. However, almost everyone is a procrastinator and waits until the last minute to do anything. Even if their lives depend on it…they wait until the last minute.

Denial will be the killer of many a person. Nobody thinks bad things can happen to them, until THAT bad thing IS happening to them. Even then, their brain will be saying this CAN'T be happening.

The point of this particular chapter is to get you to ask yourself what you will do if you find yourself unexpectedly caught in the masses of people fleeing the city.

What then? What's your plan?

When do you abandon your expertly packed, fully loaded, bug-out vehicle? I think leaving your vehicle and going on without it, for most people will not be easy. When do you abandon your vehicle?

Let's look at your options in this scenario of a major disaster event that forces people to flee the cities by the millions:

1. Your plan A, for driving to your destination is no longer a possibility.

2. Your plan B, for driving back is not an option. The roads are clogged with vehicles and desperate people. (Remember, desperate people do desperate things.)

The S.H.T.F. Art of War

3. Your plan C, for getting off the highway and taking an alternate route is not possible.

4. Plan D, staying until help arrives or traffic starts to move is probably not a safe bet for a plan.

   - Under normal conditions, in a civilized environment where services are still functioning, staying put might work.

   - However, in a catastrophic, SHTF situation where the rule of law is quickly breaking down…it may not be safe to stay put for very long.

The first thing we survivors should do is be brutally realistic about the situation we are now in and not underestimate our enemies. Self-deception and/or underestimation would be a *grave* mistake. Pun intended. This will be a situation that nobody's ever encountered before. Therefore, your brain will try to normalize the situation for you by defaulting to what it has encountered in the past.

The default program in your brain is this; traffic always eventually clears up. It's just a matter of waiting it out. So the urge to stay put will be a strong one. If you are not alone…The decision to leave the vehicle will also be met with resistance from your family members and others within your vehicle. "But we'll lose all our *stuff* except what we can carry!" Their brains will be re-booting to that same old default program consisting of what they have encountered before. The urge to stay with your vehicle will be a strong one.

The simple fact is this, being stuck in a 100, 500, or 1,000 mile traffic jam for days or even weeks might be the painful and gruesome end of you and your family. There'll be no gas, food or water and human predators will soon be looking over the herd for easy targets.

To better figure out how to defend against such dangers in transit, I use the same method I used to write this entire book. I put myself in the mindset of a bad guy and plan out how I would take advantage of the people fleeing the cities with all their goods and valuables jammed into their cars, trailers and RV's. Here's how I'd do it…if I were a bad guy. A very smart man once said "If you **know the enemy and know yourself** you need not fear the results of a hundred battles." So let's look at this from a predator's point of view:

1. All the law enforcement officials will be concentrated in the inner cities where all the worst looting and riots will currently be taking place. Based on historical fact, cell phones will more than likely not be working, as the lines of communication have become overloaded even in recent localized disasters.

The S.H.T.F. Art of War

2. The miles of highway will be virtually unguarded and phone calls to 911 will not be working. A bad guy will pretty much have free reign to commit any crime he'd like. He'll still have to be on the lookout for the stray cop car trying to make its way through the miles of jammed up roads. But the odds are very much in his favor.

3. He'll know the lay of the land ahead of time. A road atlas and other maps of his hunting area will make it much easier for him to know all the routes of travel and where the resources are for his survival.

4. He'll avoid those areas where the unprepared are alert and have formed groups and circled the wagons for protection. If he sees this kind of organization…This means that there must be someone in that group who has read this book and is armed. Or there is someone in the group who has had some kind of military training. Whatever the reason, it's not worth the risk of someone taking a shot at him…and the name of the game is risk versus reward at this point. Especially when there are so many other "non-alert" victims to choose from. He'll find it best to look for an easier target.

5. Scoped rifles, binoculars and patience will be the key to getting as much intelligence as possible on the target. Not only what kind of supplies he can liberate, but also what kind of opposition he may encounter. Taking care of or neutralizing that opposition from a distance will be the first order of business. The vast majority of preppers and survivalists think they'll encounter a fair fight. That won't be the way it will go down, kids. You'll never hear the bullet that kills you.

6. Like a lion or a wolf, a bad guy or group of bad guys will look for the easiest "pickings" on the outskirts of the herd. They'll look for your blind spot or a weakness in your defenses. It won't be a fair fight. They will wait and watch for right opportunity and when the time is right…they will strike fast so as to not allow their victims time to react. If you're a male and holding a weapon, you'd be the predator's first target.

7. There is always safety in numbers. Your best bet is to make some new friends out of the people who are in the immediate area of your section of the traffic jam. Let's hope some of them are armed citizens. The more

battle buddies you have, the safer you'll be. Because, it'll be dark soon and they mostly come at night...mostly. (a reference from the movie Aliens)

8. Like I said before, making the decision to leave your vehicle will be an extremely difficult one. When to do that will depend on the particular set of circumstances you find yourself in. It would be impossible for me to cover all the variables here. I say again and again in this book that your ability to adapt to your changing environment and to not be too rigid in your survival plans will be the most important survival tool to have.

I said there is safety in numbers. However, there is also a whole new set of difficulties that go with a group dynamic. As always, you're going to have to do what's best for you and your situation.

Staying with the group will be difficult. Everyone will want to do their own thing. They will all want to get home or get where they are going. There will be no extra food or fuel and other groups will have formed along the stretches of highway. There will be lots of competition for the resources along the routes of travel.

The social fabric will only hold up for so long before it begins to break down. When it does

Jeffrey M. Olson

break down, it will come apart at 200 miles per hour. Leaving your vehicle as soon as possible and getting a head start on the herds of survivors might also be your best bet to avoid this trouble. Maybe you can join up with a group heading in the same direction as you. Remember everyone will be out for themselves during this early stage. Everyone will have an overwhelming urge to get home or find loved ones.

Once you have made the decision to leave your vehicle, you are now on foot. Congratulations! You are now officially a scavenger and a looter. Personally, I can't rule out what I won't do to survive and feed my family if I'm starving and desperate. I've been hungry before but never starving. It's easy to say what we would or wouldn't do, with a belly full of food.

Here's something else to keep in mind. Like it or not, your 72 hour bug-out bag and battle rifle now make you a target for every other starving refugee scavenger. You'll have stuff they want. Have a concealable or collapsible firearm; and an unassuming, non-tactical backpack should also be a consideration.

As the gravity of the situation sinks in after a day or two, the highway people will begin to leave their vehicles and spill out into the countryside and small towns for help.

The S.H.T.F. Art of War

The small towns will initially lend a helping hand. But as the situation grows worse and the number of refugees gets larger, the townsfolk will eventually become overwhelmed and have to turn people away. As the situation grows more desperate and resources dry up and shipments of goods and other resources stop coming in...the townsfolk will eventually set up roadblocks and use force to protect themselves.

Being one of the first refugees to arrive in a town will have its advantages. The "first come, first served" rule will apply. Evaluating your situation fast and making the decision to leave the road you're trapped on before everyone else, will get you ahead of the thousands of others who will wait until the last minute to do anything.

I hope this gives you something to think about; especially if you are driving somewhere this summer for a vacation or passing through a densely populated area in your travels.

Jeffrey M. Olson

Part 4
The Lost Art of Scavenging.

This section will help you endure a natural, manmade disaster or alien invasion. Our current infrastructure that supplies food, power and resources is efficiently streamlined—and also very fragile. A long term disruption in those life giving resources will lead to civil unrest. It is said that we are only 9 meals away from complete anarchy.

The following information covers items and helpful strategies on scavenging to maintain your wellness potential during a societal/economic collapse. If the area you are living in is **Without the Rule of Law**, the danger increases immensely. No matter how much food you stash away for such an event, your supplies will eventually run out and you'll have to resort to scavenging to survive.

Highly Recommended Items to include in your apocalyptic scavenger survival kit

A firearm & Ammunition

Knife

Flashlight with Extra Batteries

Medium size Crowbar

- *Can be used as a weapon as well as in "entering" dwellings to scavenge for food and other items to aid in your survival.*

Leather work gloves

Safety Glasses

3M-type Dust mask

Duct Tape

Binoculars

A pair of 2-way Radios

Backpack

First Aid Kit

Rope or 550 para-cord

Ten Everyday Survival Rules

1. Always be aware of your surroundings.

    - *If you don't see the threat coming, it won't matter…to the threat.*

2. Know where all the exits are at all times…and where you can create a new one in an emergency.

    - *Always leave yourself a way out. Whether it's walking down the street or in traffic.*

3. Trust your gut feeling…but educate your gut.

4. You're most vulnerable when leaving and entering a building.

5. Wear good shoes that you can run for your life in.

6. The easy way is always where the ambush will be.

7. If it's too quiet…something's wrong.

8. Knife. Always have a knife on you. A knifeless man is a lifeless man.

9. Water. Always have extra water. Always.

10. Silence will keep you alive at night.

Activities Toward Staying Alive

In a grid-down world, you'll have to think of very creative and industrious ways to stay alive. The easy life you used to live is now long gone. Get rid of your ego. You don't know what you're capable of doing until you're in a situation where you have to do it.

You'll now have to work hard to produce and grow vegetables, fruit, dairy and meat. It takes great effort to hunt and trap animals for food and process their pelts of fur. If you can't do any of

The S.H.T.F. Art of War

that, you'll have to scavenge and salvage items for trade with the people that do.

Dumpster diving and combing the streets on trash day are activities already in common practice today, for a thrifty subculture of urban survivors.

Scavenging is a resourceful, adaptive method of survival. Scavenging means to venture out to search for and acquire goods and resources which have been abandoned, lost, left behind or overlooked by others. Scavenging will take you back through a looted grocery store, warehouse or abandoned office building long after a societal collapse. It will be a dirty and dangerous job, usually paying for its risk only in small installments.

As a scavenger, you must do your homework. For your safety you must research and observe a potential target area and verify that it is not inhabited by a criminal element. It's always best to avoid direct contact with any other survivors scavenging through an area. They will be territorial and likely to use deadly force to drive you off their area of operation.

The best locations for scavenging

It goes without saying that businesses, retail stores and warehouses will be the best places to look for goods. However, everything will already have been picked over by looters, bandits and other scavengers. You'll have to think outside the box and look beyond—and behind— the obvious. People are sneaky. Be on the lookout for hidden areas where people might have stashed items away. Check all your target locations for false walls, hidden compartments in the ceiling and floor. Pull out drawers to look inside the cabinets and dressers. Check in air ducts and fireplaces. Don't forget the bathrooms; also especially the back of the toilet.

Look for food and supplies inside abandoned houses. But also check the garages, out buildings, basements, attics; and the gardens for produce. Don't forget to look for signs of recently buried caches of valuables in abandoned yards.

Booby traps/IED's will be exceedingly rare in unoccupied scavenging areas, but remember their possibility.

A very smart scavenger will intimately know the area he or she currently lives in. Maps may be hard to come by after a societal collapse. Having a detailed map of the area in which you live now and knowing where the good scavenging locations will be ahead of time (pre-collapse) will be a big plus for you. Do your homework now. Go get a map.

The S.H.T.F. Art of War

Tools of the scavenger

Scavenging means traveling light and fast. A powered vehicle makes travel quicker and you can carry larger loads. However it will attract unwanted attention. Gasoline may also be in short supply and become an added expense to your scavenging operation. You may want to consider a two-wheeled cart that is commonly used by hunters to pull large game out of the woods.

On a big find it may be necessary to stash some items you can't carry and come back later. Think ahead and make a mental list of not-so-obvious hiding places. Also, a bag of some type for your carry-off liberated items, like a good backpack, works well. Don't leave anything behind that you can't live without—but remember, getting out empty to scavenge another day is better than not getting out at all.

A scavenger never leaves for a night of work without a pry bar along with a multi-tool and knife. Having lock picking tools and lock picking skills would be a bonus; however, in a post-collapse environment a pry bar works wonders. Leather work gloves, face mask and goggles are useful, especially the gloves.

You have got to see what you're doing. An LED

Flashlight or head lamp will help you see what you are doing. *Remember that light will attract attention.*

Bring a scavenging buddy

It is always best to work with a post-apocalyptic combat buddy when scavenging, for safety, communications and for ease of effort. Whether it's to lift a heavy object or cover a larger area in a short time, going with more than one scavenger as a team is a smart choice. If you are buddy-rich and in a high-risk area consider posting a watch.

Drones

Here's something to keep in mind while you are on one of your scavenging excursions. The United States government currently uses very sophisticated unmanned drones to survey landscapes and keep an infrared eye on borders and bad guys. In a grid-down, collapsed world, you can be sure someone will still want to know what's going on out in the apocalyptic landscape. And, also, suddenly or repeatedly sighting a new drone over your favorite scavenging turf means either you are about to compete with a very powerful apocalyptic warlord or FEMA is extremely interested in something you might be missing—or in you.

Part 5
Apocalyptic Professions.

When the infrastructure of the country has collapsed and is non-functioning, the stores will be empty and no new deliveries of goods or services will be arriving. Also, you will not be able to drive the good old caravan to the professional building and get your blood pressure check up, your flu shot, your kid's orthodontics visit and your med refill. In these primitive conditions the skills of a doctor, nurse, or dentist will be of the highest value. In the same way, having been a soldier or having knowledge of survival and bush craft skills are great talents to go along with your supply of beans, bullets and band aids. The important message of these specific cases, however, is that to be a real asset to a survival group or community rebuilding after a societal collapse, you'll need to bring more than your bug out bag and tricked out assault rifle. You'll need to bring something more substantial to the survival community or group—a specialized survival skill.

In almost every disaster, there are unprepared individuals who survive just fine. In fact, recent studies find that regular people do better than we think they do in life-and-death situations. Therefore, when preppers and survivalists emerge from their bunkers and bug out locations, they are going to be considered by the majority of "normal-folks" survivors as selfish individuals who won't share. Selfishness will be a quality that will be disliked by the masses of unprepared survivors who now surround the preppers and survivalists.

You will be outnumbered by the unprepared. Starving survivors won't like being told "I told you so" by a nut job with a rifle, chewing on an energy bar. To better understand this, I highly recommend that you watch the old "Twilight Zone" Episode called "The Shelter." It would behoove those folks who were better prepared for the disaster to now adopt a "How can I help?" attitude. Never prejudge or underestimate the survivor you help during their time of need. Forming alliances in this apocalyptic landscape will be essential to your long-term survival.

In a collapsed world that's reliving the dark ages, there will be plenty of needs to fill, other than beans, bullets and band aids. In no particular order, I have compiled a list of post-apocalyptic professions for you to consider. Make an effort to at least get a jump-start education, if not exhaustive training, in one of them.

Farmer

Farmers understand livestock and the growing seasons. They have intimate knowledge of the land and what crops you can grow. Raising livestock and growing crops for food will be vital to a community's survival.

Shepherd/Cowherd

I believe this profession will come back during a grid-down society that's been thrust back into the middle ages. There'll be a demand for trustworthy individuals to watch over the flocks/herds to ensure safety from predators…of various kinds. I think former soldiers will excel at this profession. Defending freedom and guarding the sheep and steers come naturally to the men and women who've been GI Janes or Joes.

Gardener, Botanist, Herbalist

Like farmers, the individuals who have knowledge of gardening and the many uses for plants and herbs will be a high value asset. There are medical uses for certain plants, flowers, and fungi. Being someone who has such knowledge will secure your value in a society where modern medicine has been pushed into a primitive state. Anyone who has tried their hand at gardening can attest to how easy it is not. Tending a simple garden can be a full time job.

Well Digger

In a post-apocalyptic landscape, water will be highly valued. It will be a must to have someone in the community with the knowledge to find water and the tools to dig a well. Your survival odds drop into the single digits if you can't get water out of the ground for consumption and irrigation of crops.

Engineer

I'd say most people do not have the basic, scientific, economic, social and practical knowledge needed to design, build and maintain structures, machines, devices, systems, materials and processes. You can write your own ticket in any community rebuilding a post-apocalyptic world if you are an engineer.

Cobbler or Shoe Maker

People with feet are always going to need shoes and boots. When the shoe factories are closed and people are putting a lot more miles on their feet, shoes are going to wear out faster. You'll be in high demand if you can make and repair footwear. A shoe repair specialist also repairs tarps as well.

Seamstress and Tailor

Just like shoes, clothes will be in short supply. You'll be very popular if you're an individual who can repair and produce quality garments for the harsh environments where hard work is the new law of the land. I suspect the simple tunic of the Viking age will once again be in style.

The S.H.T.F. Art of War

Trapper

Animals will not only be used as food. Their skins will once again be in high demand to make clothes and footwear. I doubt you'll hear any animal rights activists complaining during the lean times of a societal collapse or global depression.

Bait Shop Owner

Fishing will be an excellent way to add protein to your survival diet. Buying bait from an individual with a bait shop will increase your chances toward a more successful fishing trip. Owning that bait shop will ensure you have needed goods to trade with during those lean times. You'll also hear where all the best fishing spots are located.

Knife maker

My motto has always been this: "All you really need in life is a good knife and a good plan." Knife makers will be working overtime to keep up with the demand for quality cutting implements during a time where there are no more outdoor sports stores to procure any. You write your plan yourself, after reading this book.

Blacksmith/Metal Worker

When the pioneers first settled America, the blacksmith was more important than the country doctor to a settlement. The blacksmith made and repaired all the steel tools used on the farms, including even the nails for the buildings. There used to be as many blacksmith shops in towns as there were gas stations. This 4,000 year old trade will be just as important as it once was, during a post-apocalyptic rebuild of society.

Moonshiner

Alcohol has never been without value. It's always a high value item. Even in the most desperate of times, people still buy, sell and trade alcohol.

Candle Maker

In a grid-down environment where electricity is unreliable or nonexistent, a candle to light the night will be invaluable. Since it's an item that consumes itself, a person who makes candles or lanterns will have an item that will be in constant demand.

Bowyer and Fletcher

In a complete societal collapse, I believe ammo will be hard to come by and so valuable that people will not even be trading it for goods and services. It will be hoarded for emergencies only. The same will go for the modern bows and arrows. These items will mean life to a family trying to survive and will be guarded with their lives.

The lost art of making traditional bows and arrows will surge back into importance. Modern compound bows are made of modern synthetic

The S.H.T.F. Art of War

materials and moving parts. These modern parts will eventually wear out and break. In a post collapse environment where these modern bow parts are no longer made, you won't be able to replace that broken part easily. These modern bows will become useless and eventually be of little value compared to traditional archery equipment. Being a craftsman who can supply these traditional bows and arrows will make you a very popular person indeed.

Gunsmith

Firearms and replacement parts for firearms will be extremely hard to come by in an apocalyptic landscape. Having the ability to repair and make parts for broken firearms will earn you a valuable apocalyptic reputation. You might even get a nickname like "Master Blaster", the guy who can get a broken blaster up and blasting again.

Muzzle Loader Specialist

I say muzzleloader specialist and not a gunsmith or firearms specialist for very important reasons. Even though modern center fire rifles are very prevalent right now, there's been a severe run on ammunition and reloading supplies. Recent attacks on the 2nd amendment by politicians have incited a market panic on fire arms and ammunition, which in turn caused many individuals to adopt hoarding behaviors. Reloading equipment is getting more expensive and certain

Jeffrey M. Olson

components like primers are not as prevalent as they once were. It's unknown at this writing if or when the market can ever catch up with the increasing demand of the panicked populace.

In a long term grid-down scenario, where ammunition is being horded and no new ammunition is being made in vast commercial quantities, the supply will eventually run out. For these reasons, I believe the older flintlock style black powder rifles may become more common among hard core survivors. I'm referring to the type of black powder rifle you would see during the American revolutionary war. Not the modern "in-line" muzzle loader being made now.

I do realize that muzzle loading pistols and rifles using black powder are no match in a gunfight with someone using a semi automatic, high powered rifle. However, they may prove to be more versatile in the post-apocalyptic long run. Modern center fire and rim fire guns require a metallic cartridge to function and are useless without that cartridge. A muzzle loading firearm requires a lead ball, black powder and flint or cap for ignition. A person who has the ability to make black powder, melt and cast lead balls for these ancient firearms would be of great value to someone owning this type of weapon.

Teacher

I know it seems like a cliché but it's still true. Our children are the future. Education will still be the key to rebuilding a better world. The more educated you are the less likely you can be fooled. Teachers will be of great value to a group or community as they rebuild a society. Teachers who can teach multiple subjects will be most valuable.

Soap maker

Bad hygiene can lead to sickness, disease and death. A simple bar of soap would have great value when the supermarket stores become empty and looted. Making all natural, homemade soap is not difficult and a common product at every roadside craft sale these days. A wise individual would do well to peddle these hygienic bars of goodness in a broken landscape.

Laundry Washer

This profession goes along with the soap maker. In a grid-down society, an enterprising person who's set up to do the laundry of others will be an asset to communities with few resources.

Jeffrey M. Olson

Potter

There'll initially be plenty of burned out buildings and trash piles to get cups, plates and other household utensils. However, making new uncontaminated pottery for the apocalyptic masses could become a new full time profession.

Brothel Owner

The world's oldest profession has been a part of every civilization since the dawn of man. Prostitution is still making people money on every continent today.

Trading Post Master

In the past, trading posts in general were of great importance. Trading posts were not only places for buying, selling and exchanging goods. They were places for people to meet and exchange the news of the world or simply the news from their home territory. In a world where the internet and other forms of information are non-existent, these new trading posts along routes of travel will be hubs of activity. Owning one of these trading posts, in the right location, will put you in the midst of information and in the middle of the flow of trade goods.

During the California gold rush, most of the money wasn't made by the masses of would be miners flocking to the Sacramento Valley in early 1848.

The big fortunes were made in land speculation and services provided for the miners. Few of the men who actually toiled for gold made lasting fortunes. Even when they found large quantities of gold, they were swiftly parted from their fortunes. Who became rich? It was the storekeepers, riverboat captains, women of ill repute, laundry workers, card dealers and more.

Computer Programmer

Human beings will rebuild after a disaster. We always have. One of the first things we'll want to re-establish will be the internet. Having the knowledge to repair or program computers will be of great value to a society wanting to get back on line.

A Competent Human

If you take anything away from this section, it should be the fact that beans, bullets and Band-Aids are not a very good long term survival plan. The key to true self reliance and long term survival success requires being a competent human. In the literature of Robert Heinlein, the **competent man** or **competent woman** is a character who can do anything perfectly, or at least exhibits a very wide range of abilities and knowledge, making him a form of polymath.

*(A **polymath** (Greek: polymathēs, "having learned much") is a person whose expertise spans a*

Jeffrey M. Olson

significant number of different subject areas; such a person is known to draw on complex bodies of knowledge to solve specific problems.)

Robert Heinlein said a **competent** human could do the following.

Change a diaper - plan an invasion - butcher a hog - conn a ship - design a building - write a sonnet - balance accounts - build a wall - set a bone - comfort the dying - take orders - give orders – cooperate - act alone - solve equations - analyze a new problem - pitch manure - program a computer - cook a tasty meal - fight efficiently - die gallantly.

He said "Specialization is for insects."

The "**competent human**" concept embodies the basic tenet of Renaissance Humanism: that humans are empowered and limitless in their capacity for development; and it leads to the notion that people should embrace all knowledge and develop their capacities as fully as possible.

This is where I find that the majority of preppers and survivalists miss the mark. They focus entirely too much on stocking up on guns and gear.

"A man can do all things if he will."
— *Leon Battista Alberti*

We currently live in an age where information on anything is literally at our finger tips. There really

The S.H.T.F. Art of War

is no excuse for not self educating yourself on any number of useful topics. One of the best things you can start doing for yourself right now is to just shut off your TV and get your face away from the social networks that consume your time.

Focus on being a post-apocalyptic jack of all trades.

A quick word about food storage

During the first few weeks of a collapse, looting and riots will be rampant. Outside on the streets scavenging will **NOT** be the place to be. The worst in human nature will surface once people find out that there will be no consequence for their actions.

A 30-day supply of food and water already in your house, apartment or bug out location will help keep you safe at home while other unprepared individuals have to make a mad rush to the local Wal-Mart to fight the "hoards" of zombies to get things they need.

Staying out of sight and out of mind will be your best option. Just check Youtube "Black Friday Mobs" to see how people get trampled to death by other people trying to get a "good deal" on an ipad or a pair of Nike shoes. If people get that insane over shoes and electronics during "civilized" times, what will it be like when food and water are scarce?

Jeffrey M. Olson

You'll actually be surprised at just how fast you can build up a supply of extra food. Just pick up an extra can or two of canned goods every time you go shopping. Take time and find the dent free cans with the longest expiration date.

Don't forget water. You can never have too much water. Watch for deals on bottled water and pick up a case or two when you can, as often as you can. It would be best to invest in a water purification source for the long term.

Keep your 30-day stash a secret from others. A societal collapse is a bad thing and the simple fact is that people don't like to think about bad things. To consider the possibility that their whole way of life could change in a very short time causes discomfort in people. Humans do their best at avoiding discomfort on a daily basis. So it's easier to not think about it and poke fun at the people who do prepare for such "nonsense."

I'll say it again, keep your emergency stash on the down low, because these very same people, who say bad things can never happen to them and don't have any extra cans of beanie weenies in their cupboard, will be coming over to your place to be your new best friends when disaster strikes. Now your 30-day supply just went to 15 days or 7 days depending on how many of your new best friends come over.

The S.H.T.F. Art of War

Selfishness is normal and found in every species on the planet. In a community with abundant supplies, sharing is a good thing. However, in an environment where resources are scarce individuals who are selfish are more likely to pass on their genes than those who don't fight for such resources.

"Now remember, when things look bad and it looks like you're not gonna make it, then you gotta get mean. I mean plumb, mad-dog mean. 'Cause if you lose your head and you give up then you neither live nor win. That's just the way it is."
— The Outlaw Josey Wales

In Conclusion

If there's one thing that History shows us, it's that civilizations have risen and collapsed over and over throughout time. It's when they fall that we tend to see the ugliness of our species rise to the surface. We are arrogant to think that in modern times we are immune from this rule.

A societal collapse, for whatever reason, is not the End of the World. The sun rises in the morning after natural disasters and societies evolve and rebuild. Pushing through the denial phase of the disaster is step one. Being realistic about the dangers around you will be step two in the survival process.

Jeffrey M. Olson

Your skills, awareness, adaptability and scavenging activities will help you endure the hard times until the society you live in recovers. Tough times also bring out the best in people. Surround yourself with good, solid friends with a knack for salvaging and life is a joy. Choose your team wisely.

In a disaster of any kind, our ego is our enemy. Be honest about your limitations and don't take unnecessary chances. I believe there are things we can change and things we cannot; situations we can prepare for and situations we can't expect. There are just some situations we can't possibly foresee.

Your greatest survival weapons will be your adaptability and how fast you can react. Do the best you can to be reactive to the environment and flow with the situations you encounter. You can start training your mind now by replacing the words **"How can I?"** whenever you want to say **"I can't."**

Decide to survive. Enjoy the peace and abundance we have today. Learn how to use the tools in your survival toolbox. Gain the knowledge and skills that will make you as self reliant as possible.

Good luck and watch your back.

About the Author

Jeff has given up his former life as a war mongering, civilian contractor in the Middle East.

He continues to write and provides further insight into his S.H.T.F. literary work at

http://www.shtfartofwar.com

Made in the USA
Middletown, DE
05 April 2023